THE KINGDOM

By Ginny Seymour

EvenSong Publishing
1438 Jerome Ave
Astoria, Oregon 97103

Cover Illustrators
Tammy C. Dickson
Kevin Beeson

Layout
Vicky McGath

EvenSong Publishing

THE KINGDOM
Copyright @ 1999 All Rights reserved
Printed in the United States of America
ISBN 0-9718325-0-1

TABLE OF CONTENTS

<u>The Kingdom Prayer</u>

Our Father,

Who art in heaven,
Hallowed be thy name.
Thy Kingdom come. Thy will be done
On earth as it is in heaven.

Give us this day our daily bread,
And forgive us our debts,
As we forgive our debtors.
And lead us not into temptation,
But deliver us from evil.

For thine is the **Kingdom**,
And the **Power**,
And the **Glory**
Forever and Ever, **Amen**

Matthew 6:9-13

THE BLUEPRINT: Behold the Kingdom

Before your eyes stretches forth God's Kingdom. This text chronicles that Kingdom whose founding principle and major premise is love; God so loved the world that he gave his Son, Jesus. Jesus so loved that he freely offered his life, shedding his blood, to pay price for our sin. Then, Jesus sent to all Believers, the gift of the Holy Spirit. This one God, in his triune nature of Father, Son and Holy Spirit, reveals the Kingdom of God. To become a resident of this Kingdom each person who enters must accept Jesus, for Jesus is the only allowable point of entrance to this Kingdom.

Because it is a supernatural Kingdom, understanding this Kingdom cannot be acquired through natural means nor from the perspective of the world's teaching. In this Kingdom it is necessary to rely on the gift Jesus gives to all Believers, The Holy Spirit, the only spirit-guide to all truth.

You have been chosen, called by name from the time of your conception, to enter this Kingdom where God the Father, Jesus and the Holy Spirit have a plan for your life. Before you awaits this plan to establish hope and a future for you, set you free in body, soul and spirit. This text is designed as a blueprint - a blueprint for securing your freedom!

My intent in writing *The Kingdom* is to map the basic truths of Christian faith for the Kingdom traveler. *The Kingdom* text establishes the entry way and perimeters of the Kingdom. The text is written in a specific order for reasonable progression, with stories, teachings, directions, sample prayers, and personal experiences. *The Kingdom* is not intended to cover everything a Christian should know or believe, nor is it final, or complete. Other Christian authors have written volumes on topics, which are covered here in just a paragraph or two. Learning and applying all these principles takes time, and the guidance of the Holy Spirit.

It is with a great, *Shout of Thanksgiving*, that I dedicate this series to: Father God who loves me, Jesus, my friend and advocate, and the Holy Spirit, my beloved teacher. I wish to thank Dean and Wayne McPeak, Living Water's prayer group, Jean Rudy, Angie Nuxoll and Tamara Dickson for their acts of kindness and faithfulness, Nancy, Jen and Cindy for their prayers and support and the many others who encouraged me along the way.

I pray for you, my reader: *May the eyes of your heart be enlightened, in order that you may know the hope to which he has called you, the riches of his glorious inheritance in the Saints, and his incomparably great power for us who believe (Ephesians 1:18 - 19).*

I have been in bondage, but now am free. I have found the treasures of the Kingdom. Into your hands I now pour out these treasures. Enter now into this Kingdom of treasures – this Kingdom of everlasting love.

Ginny

THE KINGDOM COMES

In the beginning, God creates the heavens and the earth, plants and the beasts, man and woman. Out of dust of the earth he forms man and woman in his own image, breathes on them his breath of life and imparts to them dominion over all the earth. Perfect created beings dwell in the perfect created order in the presence of his Creator. And God calls all that he has created - good.

But, in his conceit, mankind forsakes his Creator and chooses to turn and listen to a wicked lie from a fallen angel. A portal of evil opens wide and disgorges its kingdom of lies, shame, fear, curses and death over innocent creation (Genesis 1 - 3:24). God, because of his holy, blameless nature, cannot dwell with evil and so opened a great, impassable chasm between God and his beloved.

This is the study of the restoration of that broken relationship and the finding of the way back to the Kingdom of God.

THE KINGDOM

God has a heavenly Kingdom and he wishes his Kingdom to be established and his will to be done on earth as it is in heaven. This Kingdom is entering into intimate relationship with God the father, Son and Holy Spirit.

He has given us a picture of his Kingdom pattern in the Biblical types from the Old Testament and in the New Testament through the words and life of Jesus and his followers. In the Old Testament God establishes Kingdom and favor relationship with Israel by the sacrificial offering for sin with the blood of an innocent lamb. In the New Testament, God the Father sends his only Son as the final and complete blood offering for sin for every man, woman and every child that will ever exist.

However, even if we enter into that intimate relationship we may not necessarily entirely understand how to live successfully because of our familiarity with sin and our self-dependency. In   opening a pathway for sin to enter the world the mind of mankind became darkened in understanding – from the moment of birth conditioned to accept worldly ways. We have watched as our family and other families pattern these ways of the world, television programs and movies tireless replicate them, world leaders and businesses practice them. As we rediscover that Kingdom path, we can easily continue to mix God's way with those worldly patterns. The pathway to understand living the Kingdom successfully must be rediscovered so we may learn to live in the very presence of God and in doing so once more gain dominion over the earth and rest for his soul.

We do not think like God so we must learn from him the pattern and how to apply it. For God says, *"My thoughts are not your thoughts, neither are your ways my ways,"* he declares. *"As the heavens are higher than the earth, so are my ways higher than your ways and my thoughts than your thoughts"* (Isaiah 55:8-9). Romans 12:2 exhorts, *Do not be conformed any longer to the pattern of this world, but be transformed by the renewing of your mind.* 1 Corinthians 3:18-20 points out, *Do not deceive yourself. If anyone thinks he is wise by the standards of this age he should become a "fool" so that he may become wise, for the wisdom of this world is foolishness in God's sight.*

The Kingdom of God is a spiritual perspective only viewed and understood when one accepts Jesus as Lord and Savior, God as Father, and the Holy Spirit as guide and teacher. Then eyes open and the Kingdom of God can be seen (1 Corinthians 2:12-15). No one can see the Kingdom of God unless he is born again (John 3:3). This Kingdom is the *only* Kingdom where long-term success, true happiness and peace for the body and soul is possible. In the world there will always be trials and tribulations, but Jesus overcame the world. By knowing God and practicing his Kingdom, great will be the benefits for the body, soul and spirit of man.

PART 2   LIVING THE KINGDOM HERE AND NOW

The Kingdom becomes alive, almost electric in and around you, a spiritual place in which you exist, move, are loved and live in relationship. You live the experience, surrounded by others on their journey and others in the world.

The concept could be compared to the "virtual reality" of being inside a computer involved in a sophisticated cyber game. You enter as an active participant, a player as it were. Your entry code is your personal relationship with Jesus. Your Bible is your map and the Holy Spirit your personal guide. It is a living, active experience in which God has developed each scenario to fit your personality, personal satisfaction and learning requirements. The Kingdom experience is played out through the circumstances, the people and the choices you make.

Each quest is designed to cause you to grow in strength and maturity. There is treasure to be discovered, battles to be won, enemies to be routed, puzzles to be solved, territory to own, captives to be set free, dangerous pits to be avoided. As your spiritual authority grows you become a mighty warrior for God and for good. God guides you personally and individually through his *rhema* and *logos* Word. He uses others in the Kingdom to help you along the way.

Kingdom people journey as community. Like Moses and the people of Israel as they left Egypt journeyed as a community. Everyone is important, needed and has a part. Not everyone is at the same level of maturity, but everyone who has a personal relationship with Jesus is living the experience.

If you conquer a troublesome puzzle or traverse a steep pathway, you reveal the trouble spot to those still struggling in the maze so that those who follow know where safe footholds and handholds are located. If someone has no legs, you place them on a stretcher and pack them to the top. You rejoice over the victory of others and you suffer, you cry, laugh, sing, and dance together. As you pass by someone in the world, you reach out a hand and share the good news of God's love with them.

You can compare the Kingdom to virtual reality games found in a computers, but these games are not reality at all, only surface entertainment. Kingdom living is reality, it is the most personal adventure possible. Kingdom living is relationship - the binding of your heart in love to Jesus and to others. Nothing satisfies your soul like Kingdom living.

This Kingdom where God offers social and spiritual relationship is more real and solid than the concrete under your feet. Concrete may appear solid, but in a few years it will crumble and decay. The Berlin Wall, dividing the former nations of East and West

Germany, appeared solid and foreboding, having been raised up and maintained by the Communists. In a day's time and to the surprise and applause of the world, it crumbled.

Many kingdoms and philosophies that have consumed minds, ruled hearts and appeared indestructible are gone from the face of the earth, existing only in history books. However, the Kingdom of God endures forever and so does God's covenant of relationship. This extraordinary offer is not obtainable, nor is it even available in other religions. This God of the Bible values life and relationship.

This is how the Word of God instructs us, *"Stand at the crossroads and look. Ask for the ancient paths. Ask where the good way is and walk in it. And, you will find rest for your souls." Jeremiah 6:16*

PART 3   THE KINGDOM AND YOU - a brief overview

WHERE IS THE KINGDOM OF GOD?
The Kingdom of God first becomes resident in you (Luke 17:21).

WHO PAID FOR THIS PRIVILEGE?
Jesus laid down his life on the cross, offering his blood as the purchase price to restore the relationship with God that Adam relinquished (Romans 5:12-21).

WHO IS ELIGIBLE FOR THE KINGDOM?
The opportunity for anyone to enter into the Kingdom of God began the moment Jesus rose from the dead. Jesus opened a path for every person to enter into his covenant and for everyone in every nation to know God (Luke 24:45-47, Acts 10:44-48).

HOW DO WE ENTER THE KINGDOM?
God offers this free gift of salvation to anyone who will receive it. All who receive and accept this free invitation can potentially receive all the benefits the Kingdom has to offer (Ephesians 1:3). It is through the grace of God that this invitation is extended; the privilege cannot be earned, it is a gift from God (Ephesians 2:8-9).

In this Kingdom, we become part of the family of God, his sons and daughters. A one-to-one speaking and learning relationship with the triune Godhead is established: Jesus as our Brother, God as our Father and the Holy Spirit as our counselor/teacher. Others, who have had a similar experiences, can become our Kingdom brothers and sisters (Ephesians 1:4-6).

WHAT DOES THE KINGDOM OFFER?

The Kingdom provides a relationship with the Godhead and transforming power (II Corinthians 3:18). Jesus forgives our sins (1 John 1:9). We enter into life and fellowship with God for eternity and when our physical body dies we receive a new body and enter heaven (1 Corinthians 15:42-44).

WHAT ABOUT EQUALITY IN THE KINGDOM?

In the Old Testament, Jewish kings, priests, and prophets had a special Kingdom relationship. God imparted his divine purpose through them. In the New Testament, Jesus opens the door for everyone - man, woman, child, slave or free. Equality is not struggled for or earned. Equality is already established. (Galatians 3:26-28).

HOW DOES THE KINGDOM ADVANCE?

The Kingdom advances by inviting others to receive, (Matthew 28:16-20), practicing the Kingdom for the benefit of others and ourselves (Galatians 5:22-24), and teaching others of the King and his Kingdom (Matthew 28:16-20; 2 Timothy 4:1-2).

HOW DID THIS KINGDOM COME INTO EXISTENCE?

God so loved the World that he gave his only begotten Son that whosoever believes in him should not perish but have eternal life. God did not send his Son into the world to condemn the world but through him the world might be saved (John 3:16).

WHAT ARE THE FOUNDING PRINCIPLES OF THE KINGDOM?

The founding principles are faith, love, and hope. They are the pillars upon which the Kingdom is built. However, without love, there is no Kingdom, for it is by love and through love that the Kingdom of God is established (I Corinthians 13:1-13). Love is the primary principle and force of the Kingdom; Not a wishy-washy kind of love, but a strong, powerful love, the kind of love that lays down its life as a sacrifice for others.

HOW SECURE IS THIS KINGDOM?

The Kingdom of God is an unshakable Kingdom (Hebrews 12:28). In this Kingdom an eternal God offers to mere humans ever-lasting life (Daniel 7:26-27, Isaiah 55:3, John 3:15-16).

REVIEW AND PROJECT

Chapter One recognizes both worldly patterns of living and patterns of living established by the Kingdom of God. Its premise is, at times we live according to worldly standards because these standards are familiar patterns practiced around us almost daily.

Here presented is the opportunity to move out of the principles of the kingdom of this world and step into practicing the principles of an actual kingdom called, *The Kingdom of God*. As we choose to enter into a relationship with Jesus as Lord and Savior, we can be truly set free through his Kingdom living.

The following chapters offer a panoramic view of the Kingdom of God, its length and breath, height and depth, all the way down to the very fabric of its being. It reviews Kingdom organization, how different elements of the Kingdom function, how to become a part of God's eternal Kingdom, the rights and privileges of being a Kingdom member, practical applications of Kingdom principles of love, faith and hope, along with Kingdom healing. Throughout the study there are opportunities for prayer.

Enter now into viewing this Kingdom based on love - the un-shakable eternal Kingdom of the one, true, triune God.

CHAPTER 2   THE EVERLASTING KINGDOM
PART 1   THE TRIUNE GOD

THE EVERLASTING KINGDOM

To understand the Kingdom of God one must first grasp the overall structure of his Kingdom. This chapter begins with a scripture study on who God is. Here you will also view his heavenly angels and the eternal life - a large overview of his heavenly Kingdom and what it offers man.

THE TRIUNE NATURE OF GOD

Christians recognize God as triune: Father, Son and Holy Spirit. Each part of the trinity has a different personality, attributes and functions, but there is only one God. This God lives outside of our time line although he is the Creator of time. He is above and beyond the limits of this world and the limits of our earthly imaginations.

God the Father is: the great I Am, Creator of the Universe, the Holy One of Israel. He is our omnipresent, omnipotent, Abba father who created us in his very image. This eternal God rests upon his sapphire throne in heaven surrounded by his rainbow glory and angelic beings worship around his throne day and night, night and day (Ezekiel 25-28).

GOD THE FATHER

- ❑ Is one God   Deuteronomy 6:4
- ❑ Is the only God   John 17:3
- ❑ Reigns   Psalm 9:7, Psalm 47:6-9
- ❑ Is living   Jeremiah 10:10, Revelations 4:9
- ❑ Is holy and eternal   Revelation 4:8
- ❑ Is love   1 John 4:8; 4:16   His love endures forever Psalm 118:1-4
- ❑ Created the heavens and the earth   Genesis 1:1
- ❑ Is almighty   Genesis 17:1
- ❑ Inspired every Scripture   2 Timothy 3:16
- ❑ His Word stands forever   Isaiah 40:8
- ❑ Never sleeps or slumbers   Psalm 121
- ❑ Is the source of all creation and all wisdom   Proverbs 8

❏ Rewards those who seek him   Hebrews 11:6
❏ Is awesome   Deuteronomy 7:21, 10:17
❏ Is righteous   Psalm 11:7
❏ Judges   Hebrews 12:23
❏ Is full of compassion   Psalm 116:5-6
❏ Is jealous and avenging   Nahum 1:2-3
❏ Tests hearts   I Chronicles 29:17
❏ Forgive sins   Mark 2:7, 1 John 1:9
❏ Turns our darkness into light   Psalm 18:28
❏ Laughs at the enemy   Psalm 2:4
❏ Is a consuming fire   Hebrews 12:28-29
❏ Disciplines every son (and daughter) he accepts   Hebrews 12:5-6
❏ Makes all things possible   Matthew 19:26
❏ Poured out his love   Romans 5:5
❏ Is faithful   Deuteronomy 7:9
❏ Does not show favoritism   Romans 2:11
❏ Loves the world, gave his only Son so Believers would not perish, but have eternal life   John 3:16
❏ Has made us to be heirs and co-heirs with Christ   Romans 8:17

THE TRIUNE GOD

Jesus, the Son of God, is: the Kings of Kings and Lord of Lords, the Savior of the World, the One who was, and is and is to come, the One who holds the keys to the Kingdom of Heaven (Matthew 16:19) and the keys to Death and Hades (Revelations 1:18) in his hand and our soon coming King. He stands at the right hand of the throne of God the Father (Acts 7:55). God the Father has placed all things under his feet, given him all authority and appointed him head of the church (Ephesians 1:22) and commanded all his angels to worship him (Hebrews 1:6). He is the Light of the World, and nothing, neither death nor life, angels or demons, the present or the future, any powers, neither height or depth nor anything else in all creation can separate us from his love (Romans 8:38-39).

GOD THE SON

❏ One with the Father   John 17:22
❏ Is part of the triune Godhead   John 17:21
❏ Was present at Creation   John 1:1-10, 14
❏ Is the Light of the World   John 8:12
❏ The Son of Man   John 3:13 (see footnote)
❏ The Son of God   Luke 1:30-35   Is God's only Son   John 3:16

- ❑ The only way to God the Father   John 14:6
- ❑ The only way to salvation   Acts 4:12
- ❑ Our sin offering   Romans 8:3
- ❑ Chose us and adopted us   Ephesians 1:4-5
- ❑ Is the Word of God   John 1:1-4   Revelations 19:11-16
- ❑ Is the Lamb of God that takes away the sin of the world   John 1:29
- ❑ Gives eternal life   John 3:16
- ❑ Is the Gate   John 10:7
- ❑ Our Shepherd   Psalm 23, John 10:4
- ❑ Is gentle and humble of heart   Matthew 11:29
- ❑ Is the Bread of Life   John 6:35
- ❑ Is the Lion of the Tribe of Judah   Revelation 5:5 (see footnote)
- ❑ Is the Captain of the Hosts of Heaven   Revelation 19:11-16 (see footnote)
- ❑ Is the Resurrection and the Life   John 11:25
- ❑ Is the hope of the nations   Matthew 12:18-21
- ❑ Heals the sick   Matthew 4:23-24   Commands us to heal   Mark 16:17
- ❑ Baptizes in the Holy Spirit   Matthew 3:11
- ❑ Is the same yesterday, today and forever   Hebrews 13:8
- ❑ Was conceived by the Holy Spirit   Matthew 1:20
- ❑ Was born of a virgin   Luke 1:26-35
- ❑ Was baptized in the river Jordan by John the Baptist   Mark 1:9
- ❑ Was Holy Spirit-empowered, tempted, healed the sick and blind, preached and proclaimed the Kingdom of God: Gospels of Matthew, Mark, Luke and John
- ❑ Was buried and rose on the third day, breaking the power of death over mankind Luke 24:1-7; Luke 24:45-47; 1 John 5:11-12
- ❑ Is Alpha and Omega, the First and the Last, the Beginning and the End Revelations 22:12-13
- ❑ Is returning soon   Revelations 22:7,12

TRIUNE GOD

The Holy Spirit is the gift of God to us - the very life-force of God come to dwell within man (Acts 1:4) releasing though man gifts (Romans 12:1-11) and the very character of Jesus (Galatians 5:22-23). The Holy Spirit sovereignty determines which gifts each Believer should have. He is the only Spirit of Truth and the God appointed teacher - the revelator of Jesus. He is the power force that delivers and sets us free.

GOD THE HOLY SPIRIT

- ❏ Is the third person of the triune God   Matthew 3:16 (see footnote)
- ❏ Is the breath of God   John 20:21-23
- ❏ Spoke through the Old Testament kings, priests and prophets Samuel 16:13, Luke 1:1-23,67, Ezekiel 2:1-2 (see footnote)
- ❏ Anointed Jesus for ministry   Luke 4:16-21
- ❏ Conceived Jesus in the womb of Mary   Matthew 1:18
- ❏ Descended like a dove upon Jesus at the Jordan River   Matthew 3:16-17
- ❏ Is the Spirit of God   Matthew 3:16 (see footnote)
- ❏ His coming was predicted by Jesus   Acts 1:4-5
- ❏ Empowers the Believer   Acts 1:4-8
- ❏ Is the Teacher   Luke 12:12
- ❏ Is the Spirit of Truth and guide to truth   John 16:13-15
- ❏ Is the Counselor   John 14:15-16
- ❏ Was present at creation   Genesis 1:2
- ❏ Appeared as wind   Acts 2:2-3
- ❏ Appeared as tongues of fire   Acts 2:1-4
- ❏ Manifests gifts in the Believer   1 Corinthians 12:1-11
- ❏ Can be grieved   Ephesians 4:29-30
- ❏ Is the promised gift   Acts 2:14-18
- ❏ Is our overflowing hope   Romans 15:13
- ❏ Brings the gift of prophesy   Joel 2:28
- ❏ Speaks in dreams and visions   Joel 2:28
- ❏ Enables men to speak with other tongues   Acts 2:1-4
- ❏ Is a gift to the Jew and the Gentile Believer   Acts 15:6-9
- ❏ Does not speak on his own but only what he hears Jesus speak   John 16:12-13
- ❏ Is the promise for Christians and their children   Acts 2:38-39
- ❏ Enables the Believer to speak with boldness   Acts 4:31
- ❏ Exhibits fruit through the Believer   Galatians 5:22-25
- ❏ Is given to the church to produce signs, wonders, miracles, healing, deliverance, conviction of sin, and release preaching. The Book of Acts

PART 2   ANGELS

What are angels and what is their role in the Kingdom?

Angels are supernatural beings created by Jesus that move freely between heaven and earth. They exist in the same supernatural realm as God These power-filled beings of light are God's assistants (Colossians 1:16) in the battle to establish his Kingdom. Their role in the Kingdom is to serve and minister to God, and safeguard and minister to his people (Hebrews 1:7). They can appear in human form to assist people (Genesis 19:1), but are not be worshipped. They were created to actively participate with man in the battle to establish God's Kingdom.

ANGELIC FUNCTIONS

◆ Angels Worship (Revelation 4:6-8)
Angels worship at the throne of God.

◆ Angels Deliver Messages (Matthew 1:20, Luke 1:6)
Gabriel is the highest-ranking Messenger Angel.

◆ Angels Minister (Hebrews 1:14, Acts 12:7-10)
Angels minister to people in time of need and can deliver them from danger.

◆ Angels Battle over Territories (Daniel 10:12-13)
Michael is the highest-ranking Warrior Angel.

◆ Angels Guard (Revelation 2:1, Psalm 91:11, Psalm 34:7)
Angels guard children, adults and churches.

Fallen Angels: One third of the angels created by God revolted and chose to leave the presence of God. They are referred to as: Satan, demonic forces, forces of darkness. They can appear as angels of light to deceive people into following a way other than the true way - Jesus. They are allowed authority because of Adam's sin. They cannot maintain authority over a Christian who chooses to follow Jesus. A short study of fallen angels is found in Christian Primary III, *The Power*.

God has prepared eternal fire for the devil and the fallen angels (Matthew 25:41). But his Word speaks often of the glorious role of angels on God's side. These angels are highly visible in the prophetic book of, *Revelations*. There are legions of them (Psalm 68:17 see footnote and Matthew 26:53)! The following Bible story poignantly reveals large numbers of angels in their role of guarding and protecting. Believe that God can open your eyes to see the work of his angelic force as he opened the eyes of Elisha's servant.

ANGELS, THE CHARIOTS OF FIRE

Time and time again Elisha, the man of God, warned the king of Israel to be on his guard against the king of Aram. Enraged, Aram summoned his officers and demanded of them, "Will you not tell me which of you is on the side of the king of Israel?"

"None of us, my Lord," said one, "but Elisha the prophet tells

the king of Israel the very words you speak in your bedroom." So the king sent horses, chariots and a strong army force to the city of Dothan. They went by night and surrounded the city. When the servant of Elisha arose the following morning he was stunned by the surrounding horses and chariots of war.

"Oh my lord, what shall we do?" The servant asked Elisha.

"Do not be afraid," the prophet answered. "Those who are with us are more than those who are with them." And, Elisha prayed. "Oh Lord, open the eyes of my servant so he may see!"

Then the Lord opened the servant's eyes. He looked and saw the hills full of horses and chariots of fire all around Elisha (2 Kings 6:16-25).

Angels were there to supernaturally guard Elisha because Elisha was a man of God. God has assigned to all his people these powerful unseen warriors (angelic forces).

PART 3   ETERNITY

Eternity is that state of existence prepared for us by the Father, an actual, glorious, everlasting place where man steps out of time and steps into living eternally, joyfully, permanently and supernaturally where God lives. This section reviews those areas of the Kingdom dealing specifically with eternity.

THE CROSS

The cross, the pivotal point of all history, is the most important symbol of the Kingdom and of eternity. It is the victory upon which the entire Kingdom rests. Jesus was crucified and his blood shed for the forgiveness of our sin on the cross. The work of the cross opens the door for the Believer to enter eternal life. The blood that was shed upon a cross redeems a world that is lost. Jesus died and rose again and his death and resurrection prepares a way for us.

ETERNAL LIFE

Eternal life is a free gift, paid for by the blood of Jesus. On a cross Jesus erased for man the penalty of sin. For Jesus has spoken, *"I am the resurrection and the life. He who believes in me will live, even though he dies; and whoever lives and believes in me will never die." (John 11:25)*

When you accept Jesus as Lord and Savior, you receive this free gift of eternal life. At that instant you enter into eternal life.

DEATH

What then is physical death if we are to live eternally? The physical body will die. At death the person's soul and spirit enter into heaven, where they receive a new body - one that never dies. This is the entrance into everlasting life. Those left behind on earth experience sorrow because of the resulting separation. They can, however, look forward to great joy when they are reunited with loved ones in heaven for eternity. Death loses its grip over man when he becomes an eternal creature.

Where, oh Death, is your victory? Where, oh Death, is your sting? 1 Corinthians 15:55

THE LAMB'S BOOK OF LIFE

How does God know if a person is to receive eternal life? God keeps a record in heaven containing the names of those who have chosen Jesus as their Savior (Revelations 3:10, 21:27). This record is called *The Lamb's Book of Life*. Whenever anyone has their name in *The Lamb's Book of Life*, their sin has been paid for with the blood of Jesus and they can enter into the Kingdom of Heaven when their physical body dies. At that point they become part of the great cloud of witnesses who cheer for those still living on earth as we persevere and run the race marked out for us (Hebrews 12:1 see footnote).

If a person's name is not in the Lamb' s Book of Life, their own sin condemns them to eternal separation from God, in the lake of fire - a place of everlasting torment (Revelation 20: 11-15).

PRAYER

Prayer is that eternal conversation between God and man about eternity. It is making substance of the Kingdom here on earth.

Prayer can take on many forms, such as, prayer requesting: forgiveness, blessing, protection, healing, personal needs or intercession for friends, cities, and nations. You can pray the prayer of confession of faith, a prayer of thanksgiving, or a prayer of praise. Prayer can be loud. Prayer can be soft. You can be on your knees or you can be walking around a grocery store. Prayer can take many forms and can be one of the above or all of them at once. Prayer is not confined to the inside of the four walls of a Church but is an and on-going conversation with God that builds relationship. The word of God exhorts us to pray unceasingly (Ephesians 6:18) for prayer (communication) is the substance of good relationship

In the Bible, prophets pray (2 Kings 6:17). Jonah prayed from inside the belly of a great fish (Jonah 2:1). The Priests pray (Luke 1:5-17). Kings, like King David, pray (Psalm 51:10). Common people such as Hannah (I Samuel 2:1-10), Daniel (Daniel 6:10), and Zechariah pray (Luke 1:11-13) and receive answers from God. The disciples pray (Acts 4:31) and Jesus prays (Mark 1:35).

Psalms 32:6 challenges us, *Let everyone who is Godly, pray.* I Thessalonians 5:16-18 states, *Be joyful always, pray continually, give thanks in all circumstances.* Ephesians 6:18 exhorts, *Pray in the Spirit continually.*

Prayer is such an integral part of the Kingdom experience, it is the air one breathes. Jesus gave us this model in the Lord's Prayer to teach us how to pray (Matthew 6:9-11).

HEAVEN

Here on earth, our physical body just wears out. But God has offered eternity to man with the best retirement plan ever in an astounding place called heaven. And it is free!

Heaven is the eternal, holy dwelling place of God (Deuteronomy 26:15), the Creator of heaven and earth (Genesis 1:1, 14:19). God bestows citizenship in heaven (Philippians 3:20) and prepares a place for the Saints of God (those whose names are written in *The Lamb's Book of Life*). The Believer will dwell there in the presence of God — forever.

There are the heavens around the earth, the heavens of the universe and the heaven where God has his throne, his holy dwelling place (Deuteronomy 26:15). God created them all. He is a God of immense creativity. Here on earth we have been able to admire some of his handiwork.

The Word of God only hints and gives an occasional intriguing glimpse of this most splendiferous place. We know that the heaven where God rests upon his sapphire throne is surrounded by a rainbow (Ezekiel 1:26, 28). Angelic beings worship around this throne and so do men (Revelation 4:1-4, 9-11). That is where we will meet God face-to-face and worship around his throne.

The Word of God has given us some scriptural clues to aid in our concept of what heaven will be like. God made animals and the animals he made he called good. He tells us specifically there are animals in heaven. Revelation 19:11 purposely mentions horses. There are plants as Revelation also reveals - trees of life that bear fruit coming down from the throne of God (Revelation 21:2). Out of his throne also proceeds a great crystal river (Revelation 22:1 for all of us who love rivers). God has every beautiful stone known to man with pearls twelve foot in size, gold to pave the streets and walls of a city (22:2). So there is a city in heaven (Revelation 21:2).

There we will be given a new indestructible body, see the friends, family and those who have gone before us in the faith, including Old Testament prophets. God will wipe away our tears (Revelation 21:4) and give us a place of everlasting citizenship (Philippians 3:20). This place, prepared for us by God, is free. It is a place of eternal joy being in the presence of God forever and ever!

THE RETURN OF THE KING

When Jesus left his disciples almost 2,000 years ago, Jesus told them that it was not for them to know the times and the dates the Father has set (Acts 1:7). At that very same time, two angels spoke to the disciples after Jesus was taken back into heaven and encouraged the disciples saying that the same Jesus who was taken up into heaven would come back the same way they saw him go (Acts 1:10).

We are to be watchful to know that the time is coming soon for the return of Jesus. He will return to rule the nations, establish his Kingdom rule here on earth, and bring peace for 1,000 years (Revelation 20:1-3).

The exact moment of that return no one knows for sure. We can know that we live in an era close to that coming of Jesus because of the signs of the times around us.

There are many excellent Bible studies currently on the market delineating the soon return of Jesus. I recommend to my reader to buy several and study them. Until the return of Jesus we are to live our lives watching and praying for his return.

CHAPTER 3   THE KING AND HIS KINGDOM
PART 1   JESUS THE KING

JESUS THE KING

Now you have seen the overview of the eternal Kingdom of God. Here Jesus stands before you offering you eternity. It is the way of the Kingdom that you must enter here. It is a choice of kingdoms: the kingdom of darkness or, the Kingdom of light. And you must choose. A lack of choice leaves you inheriting the kingdom of darkness. God's desire is that you choose his Kingdom. *For God so loved the world that he gave his one and only Son, that whoever believes in him shall not perish but have eternal life. For God did not send his Son into the world to condemn the world, but to save the world through him (John 3:16-17).*

The Kingdom has the Word of God (The Bible) written by prophets of God. Jesus is that Word of God made flesh (John 1:1-14). Jesus is that living Word that makes a contract with man and signs it in his blood.

THE KING'S INVITATION

Jesus sends forth his invitation to all the world - to any who would hear and respond.

Come to me, *all you who are weary and burdened, and I will give you rest. Take my yoke upon you and learn from me, for I am gentle and humble in heart, and you will find rest for your souls. For my yoke is easy and my burden is light (Matthew 11:28).*

If anyone is thirsty, *let him come to me and drink. Whoever believes in me, as the Scripture has said, streams of living water will flow from within him (John 7:37b-38).*

I am the Light of the World. *Whoever follows me will never walk in darkness but will have the light of life (John 8:12).*

OUR INVITATION TO THE KING

Dear Jesus, I am a sinner. I ask you to forgive my sin. Come live in my heart and be my Lord and King that I may live eternally with you.

Amen

By faith you receive Jesus as Lord and Savior. You step out of a kingdom of darkness and into the Kingdom of Light. Your name is now written in *The Lamb's Book of Life,* and you received the free gift of eternal life. This experience is referred to as the salvation experience - the state of acceptance of Jesus as the one who will save you.

From now on, you have an advocate with God the Father. You can confess and repent of your sin immediately to receive forgiveness and restore relationship.

If we are forgiven do we then continue to sin? No! While we no longer need to be slaves to sin (Romans 6), we must always accept responsibility for and confess our sin. As *we are faithful to confess our sin, he is faithful to forgive.*

To deny we sin, or to pass the blame on to others is rebellion. Rebellion is linked to the sin of witchcraft (1 Samuel 15:12-24 see footnote on verses 15, 23 and 24).

PART 2: THE WORD

The Bible is the foundation of the Kingdom, the source for learning about God and our relationship to him. All that God the Father, God the Son and God the Holy Spirit ever speaks will always agree with the written Word. Knowing God through his Word becomes a checkpoint for our own words, visions, dreams, ideas, and directions. The Scriptures are anointed and written under the inspiration of the Holy Spirit. All Scripture is God-breathed (2 Timothy 3:16; 2 Peter 1:21).

Reading the Word is a physical act that takes commitment and needs to be a matter of regular habit. This physical action trains our mind in the ways of God. Without the physical action of opening God's Word and reading it, our minds do not hear, know, or discern the will of God (Romans 10:17). You may not recognize the counterfeit if you are not familiar with the real thing.

Learning the ways of God requires education and effort. This education, however, needs to be under the direct supervision of the Holy Spirit. The Holy Spirit inspired all Scripture, so he is the one who helps interpret it! He is the teacher - the only guide to truth. Education with our own minds or own wisdom may lead us to know theology, but it does not lead us to know God.

As part of the study of the Word of God, the following areas will be reviewed: the four Gospels, how the Word is a living Word, the difference between logos and rhema, why you should memorize the Word, and how to read the Word.

THE FOUR GOSPELS

The Book of Ezekiel speaks of the cherubim - the throne attendants. They are the four living creatures who stand before the throne of God day and night shouting, *"Holy! Holy! Holy! Holy! Holy!"*

Each of the *four has the face of a man, and on the right side each has the face of a lion and on the left side the face of an ox. Each also has the face of an eagle (Ezekiel 1:4-12). The man, the lion, the ox, and the eagle are the symbols for the four Gospels. The four Gospels are not only written for us to read, but are so alive they stand before God's throne and shout! They are living attendants to the throne of God. Day and night they shout unto God, *"Holy! Holy! Holy! Holy!"* These four Gospels are the living diorama of the life and teachings of Jesus.

THE LIVING WORD

The Bible speaks in the past, present and future. The words are *alive,* the pages written as *a living word* from *a living God.* No other book can claim that every word written is a *living word.* The Bible stands as a book entirely different from all others. The words are not only living but they are truth and we are sanctified by them (John 17:17). They are not only words that live, but, words to live. This Word of God stands forever (1 Peter 1:25).

Scripture gives us a historical account of the struggles and travels of God's chosen people; an understanding of the relationship between God and his people; and personal comfort and support for one another via deliverance, healing, wisdom, and discipline.

Scriptures also teach and reveal coming events, and speak life into our futures.

Other texts are either based upon mankind's "wisdom," contain true stories of lives past, fiction, or are from the fields of science, medicine, or technology. No book is a living word unless it is written under the direct unction of the Holy Spirit and in full agreement with the Scriptures.

LOGOS AND RHEMA

There are two types of *living words*. One is the actual written Word on the page, *logos*. *Logos* can be read for wisdom, reference, historical perspective, or insights into the relationship between God and his people. The second type of *living Word* is called *rhema*. When a specific Scripture leaps out and you know God is speaking directly to you, you just read a *rhema* word from God. Rhema words are the divine utterances of God.

Discernment helps you recognize if a message is a Word of God for education or a Word of God for you right now. If you act upon the Word as if it is a *rhema* word, and it was really a *logos* word, you can be in for a fall.

Remember when Jesus invites Peter to walk on the water (Matthew 14:29)? What if one reads that Word and thinks they should have the power to walk on water? Unless God has spoken directly to them in a *rhema* Word they would drown or at least appear quite foolish. Differentiate between logos and rhema for yourself. Ask God and seek his confirmation!

HIDE THE WORD IN YOUR HEART

I have hidden your Word in my heart that I might not sin against you. Psalm 119:11

Memorizing a Bible passage helps change wrong patterns of thinking. If you know the *real* Word and the *real* God, you will not be easily swayed to accept counterfeits. Memorizing takes a Kingdom Word and works it into your physical reactions and into the thoughts of your heart. Hiding the word in you heart allows you to tear down the kingdom of the world that is natural to your thoughts and build a response to the Kingdom of God. When you need to take action you can respond with Kingdom thinking and reap Kingdom benefits.

Memorization provides an entrance into Kingdom living, helping us tear down worldly structures and assisting us in building on a strong Kingdom foundation.

Kingdom thinking is not just, head thinking. Kingdom thinking is also, heart thinking. Perhaps you have not considered that you think with your heart, but the Word says that *as a man thinks in his heart, so is he (Proverbs 23:7, Matthew 15:9, Proverbs 16:9).*

READING THE LIVING WORD

There are different approaches to reading the Scriptures. Some people find passages and "chew" on them, devouring and understanding one small portion at a time. Some memorize section after section, while others read several books to get the overview.

Different personality types will approach the Word differently. Insisting that everyone learn the same way ignores the fact that we were created uniquely and have different views to lend to the body of Christ. While one view is not better than another, we will tend to gravitate more towards one type of learning than another because of our personality type or because of the season of life in which God has us walking. Different perspectives allow balance and variety.

PART 3   THE CONTRACT SIGNED IN BLOOD

The Bible reveals to us the contract God has with his Kingdom people. The Bible is divided into two sections: the Old and New Testaments. This division is also known as the Old and the New Covenants. Under the Old Covenant, the sins of God's people were covered through the blood sacrifice of an unblemished lamb. Under the New Covenant, the blood covering for the forgiveness of sin is the blood of Jesus. Jesus is the Lamb, sacrificed once and for all. We appropriate this gift by asking. Jesus is our advocate with God the Father. Through him, the relationship with God the Father that was lost at *the fall of man,* is now restored.

Those of us who are Gentiles (non-Jews) are grafted into the promise of the Old Covenant and become as children of Abraham, the children of faith (Ephesians 2:11-13). God calls us his chosen people, a royal priesthood and the people of God just as he calls the Jewish people his chosen people (1 Peter 2:9) in the Old Covenant (Old Testament). We become the friends of God (John 15:14-15). Because Jesus lives in us and has paid the price for our sin, when God looks at us he sees the blood of Jesus that has paid the redemption price and we are righteous in his sight.

Two thousand years ago, Jesus, Son of God, born of a virgin, became man, and restored our relationship. Each and every citizen of the Kingdom chooses to become a citizen and come under his blood covenant. Until that choice is made, man's nature is not renewed and his nature turns toward sin. Man's true nature lies along the path of hostility towards God (Romans 8:5-7). But, through Jesus and his blood offering, we become more than conquerors (Romans 8:28-39). Because of this covenant nothing can separate us from his all consuming love, for his covenants are everlasting.

The salvation experience demands nothing but acceptance from the receiver, not good works! God's salvation stands as a finished work purchased and completely paid for by the blood of Jesus in the perfect sacrifice Jesus offered on the cross.

Jesus' sacrifice purchases certain rights and privileges for those who are under the New Covenant. These rights and privileges enable citizens of the Kingdom to be co-heirs with Jesus. We are given the right to rule and reign with Jesus (Revelations 5:10 and II Timothy 2:12). As we enter into the covenant with Jesus, all that Jesus has becomes ours. Simultaneously, all we consider belonging to us, becomes his.

POWER IN THE BLOOD

This covenant is a binding contract (solemn agreement, legal document) between God and man. It is through this blood contract of Jesus (in the New Testament) that our relationship (as Gentile Believers) with the Godhead is established.

In the Old Testament, because of the blood covenant of the lamb, the Hebrews were under the protection of God. As they kept their part of the conditions of the covenant by being faithful to God they were successful in battle, protected from disease, plagues, and from their enemies.

In Exodus 12:21-23, Moses directs the children of Israel to place the slaughtered blood of an unblemished lamb on the top and both sides of the door frames of their homes. At midnight the Lord passes over the homes of the Egyptians and the homes of the Hebrews. Judgment comes to the Egyptian homes without the blood upon the door frames, however, all under the blood are protected. The Israelites remember and still celebrate this day yearly as the day of Passover because the Lord passed over and did not permit the destroyer to enter the houses marked with the blood of the lamb.

THE NEW BLOOD COVENANT

Before Jesus was crucified, he reclined at a table to share the Passover supper with his twelve disciples. Here Jesus establishes the New Covenant in his blood - the blood of the Lamb of God.

> *Jesus took bread, gave thanks and broke it, and gave it to them saying, "This is my body given for you; do this in remembrance of me." Then Jesus took the cup saying, "This cup is the new covenant in my blood, which is poured out for you." Luke 22:19-20*

Jesus was willing to pay a staggering price for this our new covenant. He became our lamb. He sacrificed himself so that we may be under his protection. He gave his blood so that the destroyer *must* pass over and may not destroy the family under the covering of his blood. The power is in the blood that was shed - the blood that establishes our new covenant. Every time we partake in sharing this supper Jesus established, we *embrace our* covenant with him.

THE SEAL OF THE KING

Having believed, you were marked in him with a seal, the promised Holy Spirit, who, is a deposit guaranteeing your inheritance (Ephesians I:13b -14a).

THE WILL OF THE KING

KNOW that in all things, God has the power to do what he has promised (Romans 4:21).

KNOW you are not your own, but have been purchased with a price (1 Corinthians 6:20).

KNOW God has a plan and purpose for your life (Jeremiah 29:11).

"For I know the plans I have for you," declares the Lord, "plans to prosper you, and not to harm you, plans to give you hope and a future."

CLEANSE THE TEMPLE

In the Old Testament, the Glory of God dwelt in tents as his people moved from place to place. When the Israelites finally entered the Promised Land they desired to build a permanent temple for God where the Ark of the Covenant could rest and the Glory of the Lord would reside.

In the New Testament, his dwelling place is within every Christian. You offer your body to be the temple in which he abides - the temple for his Glory. You cleanse this temple so that God has a holy dwelling place, for you are to be a sacred temple, a temple dedicated totally to the Lord (1 Corinthians 3:16).

GENERAL HOUSE CLEANING

The list on the next page contains suggestions of areas that may need attention. Check these areas so you may wisely reject the ways of your enemy, Satan, and fully embrace the Kingdom. With every sin forgiven, you acquire the provision to deal with issues in effective, godly ways.

A door can be opened into a person's spirit and soul through sinful, careless, personal decisions. The enemy then has an invitation to enter and deceive until the sin is confessed and the enemy confronted and evicted.

How do you expel the unwelcome tenant? First, you name the sin and ask God for forgiveness. Next, in the name of Jesus you command that influence to go out the door through which it arrived. Pray that the opening be closed and the cross of Jesus bar the enemy from returning. Repent of the sin, cast out the deceiver, and then invite God to fill the area with his Holy Spirit.

The opportunity for cleansing is a wonderful opportunity after the salvation experience. It is also a good reference check for those who have already experienced the Baptism of the Holy Spirit. In the

Baptism of the Holy Spirit you open yourself to view and become more sensitive to the spiritual world. Areas of sin not confessed and repented of can lead to spiritual confusion and deception. (Baptism of the Holy Spirit is discussed on pages 31-33.)

Review the following list for possible ways you may have sinned, come under mind control, accepted philosophies or attempted to seek guidance for your life in ways contrary to God's Word (see Deuteronomy 18:9:13, Leviticus 19:26-32, Revelation 216-8). Add any topics you feel should be added.

❖ Lying and other specific personal sin
❖ Voodoo, hexes
❖ Spirit guides
❖ Dungeons and Dragons game or any games associated with witchcraft or occult
❖ Mind control, ESP
❖ Clairvoyance
❖ Séances (consulting the dead)
❖ Levitation, Transcendental Meditation
❖ Water witching
❖ Drugs
❖ Fortune telling, horoscope guidance, palm reading, tea leaves
❖ Racism
❖ Astral projection, telekinesis
❖ Humanistic philosophy
❖ Cults, religious legalism, religious (not godly) life-style
❖ *Karate, Martial Arts, Yoga
❖ Eastern, Asian religions, meditations, or New Age practices
❖ Pornography
❖ Sexual activity/affairs, deviant sexual behavior**
❖ Witchcraft or other satanic practices
❖ Rebellion

Objects such as the following, or books or articles on all topics mentioned above or below:

Ankhs, Buddha's/Idols
Good-luck charms, Greek gods/goddesses
"Healing" crystals
Witchcraft symbols, Horoscope signs, Egyptian Crosses
Pegasus/Fairies/Unicorns

Indian medicine bags or any objects associated with voodoo

*Pagan worship, superstition, eastern religions, meditations or phi-
losophies can train the mind in methods of thinking contrary to Scripture, and open doors of deception in the mind and heart. Some actions can be actual acts of praise to an oriental god. Check carefully
and understand fully what you are doing. You could be fully ignorant
of what is transpiring and, yet, at the same time participating in a type
of religious worship.

** Read Romans 1:24-32. Be cautious what the eyes see, the ears
hear and the heart receives as truth. A diet of television programs,
movies, music and soap operas that promote an interest and acceptance of easy sex is hazardous to your spiritual health. Cartoons that
glorify and promote interest in the occult and eastern philosophy are
hazardous to the health of your children.

We are to be a holy people, set apart to God. Therefore, we
reject those things God considers unholy: areas where we seek revelation in *any way other than through him,* or those *areas in which we
rebel against him.* He considers those areas an abomination and witchcraft, just as he did in the Old Testament. Just like his people in the
Old Testament, he will discipline us for our lack of wisdom if we follow
worldly ways.

This does not mean that everything listed above is all bad.
There are some good ideas, neat concepts, stirring sayings and high-
sounding intentions, promoted by well-meaning and nice people. But
God is a jealous God (Exodus 20:4-6). He desires that we learn from
him, practice his ways and have a heart that excludes all other philosophies and ways of worship. We not only offend God's holy nature, but when we accept something not of him we are more prone to
justifying further involvement - involvement that can lead us away
from an intimate relationship with God. Walk carefully for Hollywood
will sugar-coat white witchcraft, that is, using witchcraft for seemingly
harmless or moralistic purposes. Many, or even famous Christians,
may justify it as good because it represents doing good with good
people. Any form or use of witchcraft for any reason is strictly forbid-
den by God! There are no exceptions! It involves the supernatural
not of God and opens our spirits to serious deception by enemy
spirits.

If you are presently involved in any of these areas, or have been in the past, you may have become exposed to spiritual deception and future problems affecting your mind, will, and emotions. Praying the following prayer, as well as listening and watching for the Holy Spirit's discernment, will help you gain freedom. To remain free, you need to consciously make a commitment to stay away from these influences and remove everything related to these influences from your home.

If you fall in one of these areas again, just repeat this **Door Prayer**, perhaps with a friend. If you still need help, seek counseling, inner healing or deliverance.

DOOR PRAYER: Repeat the prayer for each area.

Lord, I confess my involvement in _____(area of sin). Forgive me for seeking revelation in any way than through you! Please continue to reveal any area in my heart where I have hidden sin, rebellion, or witchcraft. Now, in the name of Jesus, I command any deception or influence not of Jesus, that entered my life as a result of my foolish choices, to leave through the opening where you entered. In the name of Jesus, I close the door and place the cross at all openings. I invite the Holy Spirit to come and fill this place in my heart and my life. Amen!

EXPERIENCE

Usually I visualize a space with an open door and/or windows as I close my eyes to pray. I pray, commanding all influences to go out the door where they entered. In my mind I can often see shadows of things scatter and run for the open door. I always ask the person I am praying with if they have seen anything similar, most often they do. I ask them if they can see when everything has left. When they are able to say yes, or I discern all has left, (usually a fairly quick process) I then ask Jesus to bar the door and close all openings and Jesus and the Holy Spirit to come and inhabit the vacated space.

There is usually a great sense of release, relief and freedom for the person who prays this prayer. They recognize when influences leave and they no longer personally feel the draw or fascination towards those influences.

PART 2   GENERATIONAL FORGIVENESS

The cross not only has the power to break the influence of confessed sin over your life, it also has the power to stop generation curses. Sins of the family can follow in the family line. Sometimes, even illnesses can follow through family generations.

Generation curses are hindrances, negative patterns of behavior or some times illnesses that follow through generations in a family. Your forefathers could have opened a doorway to deception that allowed a negative influence to enter the family line, paving the way for evil to exist in the family. These influences can then follow family lines to the fourth generation (Exodus 20:5). Some families become so accustomed to a particular influence that they think of it as normal. For a variety of reasons, not everything immediately responds to this type of prayer. The search itself, however, can prove to be very valuable and freeing. You can ask for forgiveness for the trespasses and rebellion of your relatives, and that the rebellion and sin they passed on to you through their choices will be forgiven. You can also pray that any evil inheritance will have to change to a blessing.

Forgive the evil handed down to you in the form of words or choices. Realize it was the enemy at work, trying to destroy you. Draw a genealogy chart noting specific sins with specific parents and grandparents. Then, repent for each individual iniquity that is part of your inheritance. This may need further prayer, particularly if you do not experience complete freedom. (Deliverance is discussed in the Christian Primary III, *The Power*.)

As you study this list always keep a balance. Curses follow to the fourth generation but blessings in a family follow a family line from the thousandth generation. So, you also have many blessings through your family line. Make a list of curses and after prayer burn them up. Make a list of your blessings from your family tree and keep those.

* Divorce
* Mental illness/nervous breakdowns
* Murder/abortion/suicide
* Rejection of the Gospel
* Jealousy

- ❖ Sexual sin
- ❖ A rebellious nature
- ❖ Disabilities
- ❖ Alcohol and/or drug abuse
- ❖ Intellectualism
- ❖ Witchcraft, Wicca, (white witchcraft, witchcraft done for supposedly good)
- ❖ Some types of genetic hearing loss/genetic color blindness
- ❖ Constant debt
- ❖ Physical illnesses

ORGANIZATIONS: Masons, Job's Daughters, etc.
ABUSE: Sexual, physical, suicide, thoughts of suicide

Anything from this list, from the personal list above or nationalities* can be included in prayer. *A person's nationality can affect their decisions. Praying and placing the cross between a person's home country and themselves and praying that all influences not pleasing to Jesus stop at the cross (all positive influences to continue) is one more way to pray, we can also repent of sin for our nationality. You can also stand and forgive those who have persecuted your nationality. Jesus has already made provisions to acquire these freedoms for us, now we just make claim to our inheritance (Isaiah 53:1-12).

*CROSS PRAYER: Dear Jesus, I confess the sin of _____
(name the sin) in my family. I repent for the sin and ask you to forgive this sin in my family. Stop the power of this generation curse. I place the cross between my father and mother and their families four generations back, and command the sin, or curses, which have followed my family through the generations to stop at the cross. This iniquity is no longer my inheritance, the inheritance of my family, or the inheritance of my children. But rather blessing to a thousandth generation (Leviticus 26:40-42, Deuteronomy 7:9 Exodus 20:4-6).

EXPERIENCE

A person praying may experience a new sense of freedom and a feeling of release. Expect to see the light in the room appear brighter. Light is the symbol for life and blessing in the Old Testament (see footnotes on both Genesis 1:3 and II Samuel 22:29). The Lord will turn our darkness into light for Jesus is our light (Luke 2:32, John 1:4, 5, John 8:12).

VERY IMPORTANT MESSAGE

*The Door and Cross prayers can be used anytime but are especially important before receiving the Baptism of the Holy Spirit. The Door and Cross prayers are titled and prepared by the author and are not mentioned in Scripture.

PART 3   REPENT AND BE BAPTIZED

Peter challenged the early Church, "Repent and be baptized!" Both Peter and John the Baptist speak of two baptisms (Matthew 3:11, Acts 2: 38,39). The first baptism, a necessary act for the Believer, washes away sin. Man becomes a new creature, dead to sin and alive to Christ (John 1:4). The second baptism is with the Holy Spirit and fire (Acts 1:4; Matthew 3:11) with signs following (Mark 16:15-16, Acts 22:16) as in, The Book of Acts.

Jesus experiences both baptisms before beginning his ministry. Of Jesus' first thirty years, we know little of his activities. However, the moment Jesus is baptized in water and receives the Holy Spirit, he initiates his battle with evil and launches his ministry with signs and wonders following (Matthew 3:16-17, Mark 1:9-13).

John the Baptist preached water baptism. But the ministry of the New Testament Church begins only after the disciples receive the second baptism, the Baptism of the Holy Spirit. Both baptisms are an active part of the New Testament Church: water for the forgiveness of sin and the Baptism of the Holy Spirit for the power to live the Christian experience. They are necessary acts of faith for the Believer, one following another (Acts 2:1-17).

Those who have received Jesus as Lord and Savior already have received the Holy Spirit because God exists as one inseparable triune God. When you receive Jesus into your heart the Father and the Holy Spirit also come to abide.

When we receive Jesus he forgives all our sin. Yet, we still are to be baptized with water for the washing away of our sin. This baptism is a total immersion into Jesus, producing a new creature, dead to sin but alive in Christ.

We already have the Holy Spirit, but when we ask by faith to be baptized with the Holy Spirit and with fire, we come forth immersed in power to be a Believer.

THE BAPTISM IN THE HOLY SPIRIT

John the Baptist declared that there was one coming after him whose sandals he was not fit to carry who would baptize with the Holy Spirit and with fire. (Matthew 3:11). Before Jesus ascended back into heaven he declares in Luke 24:45-49, *"I am going to send you what my Father has promised (The Holy Spirit)."* And in Acts 1:5 *Jesus declares, "Do not leave Jerusalem, but wait for the gift my Father promised… For John baptized with water but in a few days you will be baptized with the Holy Spirit."*

When the day of Pentecost came they were all together in one place. Suddenly a sound like the blowing of a violent wind came from heaven and filled the whole house where they were sitting. They saw what seemed to be tongues of fire that separated and came to rest on each of them. All of them were filled with the Holy Spirit and began to speak in other tongues as the Spirit enabled them and signs and wonders followed. (Acts 2:1-4).

The following is a prayer to be filled with the power of the Holy Spirit. Note that some churches have an actual event called Confirmation where they pray for the release of the Holy Spirit to an individual. At that point the church has passed on this special relationship to the individual. The individual may have received the gift but never actually opened the gift they received from the church.

Below are some of the areas they can expect they have a right to enter into.

PRAYER FOR THE BAPTISM IN THE HOLY SPIRIT: Father thank you for sending your Holy Spirit! In the name of Jesus I receive the promise of the Holy Spirit. Thank you, Holy Spirit, that you are the Spirit of Truth and that you will lead me into all truth. (John16:26; Mark 16:15-18)

Jesus asked the Father to send the promised Holy Spirit: We can ask on our own behalf, or ask someone who has had the experience lay hands on us and impart the experience (Acts 19:1-6).

The first Sign: The first sign to follow is speaking in *other tongues*. This is the same sign the first church experienced in Acts 2:1-4; 19:6. Speaking in tongues is choosing to open your mouth and making an effort to produce sounds. The Holy Spirit will take over your beginning babble and you will experience a brand-new language. In faith it takes a yielding and surrendering of your tongue in making sounds. This physical action of faith allows you to accept and receive the gift being offered.

Expect: Sometime between a few minutes to a few days following your initial experience, you can anticipate your eyes to open to spiritual truths you could not understand before. In addition, a great flood of joy or emotions and an intensive learning experience often occurs. As you seek the relationship the gifts of the Spirit will follow.

Revelation and Power: The Holy Spirit reveals Jesus and the Father. Now you have received the revelation and Holy Spirit power to live successfully the Kingdom experience so go forth and possess the Kingdom (Mark 16:15-18, Matthew 28:18-20).

Signs and Wonders: In the Old Testament, revelation was evidenced through a prophet, priest or king, but today, the revelation comes as you grow in this experience. The Holy Spirit then empowers you *with gifts of signs and wonders as he did with new Believers in the book of Acts. God and his Word have not changed.*

THE JOURNEY BEGINS

Now that you have a heart relationship with Jesus, have been immersed in baptism of water and received the Holy Spirit, you are ready to begin possessing the Kingdom of God here on earth for yourself and for others.

In the following chapters, you will find methods and approaches to Godly principles. These principles are truly the foundation for Christian living. Do not expect that you can learn to apply them all at once. It is a matter of realizing the availability of these principles and beginning a life journey to apply them.

God's desire for your life is that you progress into becoming a mature believer. His Kingdom offers a firm foundation for living successfully above and beyond all the world has to offer.

Here before you stands the pillars of his Kingdom: love, faith, and hope. They are as the beacons of light to reveal the ancient pathway to God. Now step forth upon this ancient pathway and find yourself in the very heart of God's Kingdom.

STRIKING THE GROUND

To possess the Kingdom we must be persistent. The follow-ing scripture is an example to encourage us in persistent behavior.

Second Kings 13:13-19 recounts the story of the Prophet Elisha and, Jehoash, King of Israel. Elisha was suffering from the illness from which he would very soon die. King Jehoash recognized the prophet was of greater significance for Israel's military success than even Israel's military forces and so Jehoash came to see Elisha for the last time before the great prophet died.

Elisha said to Jehoash, *"take the arrows,"* and the king took *them. Elisha told him, "Strike the ground." The king struck it three times and stopped. The man of God was angry with the king and said, "You should have struck the ground five or six times; then you would have defeated Aram and completely destroyed it. But now you will defeat it only three times."* The moderate enthusiastic response to Elisha's directive reflected insufficient zeal for accomplishing the announced task (2 Kings 13:19 see footnote).

The king was advised to take his tools of war and strike the ground. But the king did it without perseverance and without zeal and so the king could only be only moderately successful in his military campaigns.

What was the purpose of the prophet asking the king to strike the ground? In the beginning all the ground belonged to God and reflected his glory. But at the fall of Adam, the ground came under a curse (Genesis 3:17-19). The ground was now where the snake crawled upon his belly (Genesis 3:14).

To restore the ground back its rightful ownership the king had to beat it with his tools of warfare in a supernatural act of faith before he could claim it in the natural. In faith he was to strike the ground beating back the curse of fear, doubt, and the lies of the snake. By relying on the supernatural (the Holy Spirit direction as given by the Prophet) he then could reclaim the land once more in the natural.

Under the New Covenant we do not choose arrows as our tools of warfare. Jesus revealed to us the way to devastate the power of the enemy and restore his Kingdom. He opened the door for the Kingdom to be restored through his example of perfect forgiveness and perfect love.

With the Holy Spirit as our guide, we use our supernatural tools to beat the land: love, forgiveness, faith, Kingdom principles, and hope. We do the supernatural action of striking the ground each time we choose the Kingdom way. We strike the ground until our actions bring forth the desired result in the natural. We persevere with the greatest of zeal in this supernatural action until the curses are broken and the victory is ours. We not only strike the ground, we beat the ground until the victory is won, for God knows that as we practice Kingdom principles, we will truly be set into an unimaginable freedom.

PART 1   BEAT THE GROUND WITH LOVE

Jesus laid down his life as the perfect blood sacrifice to cover the requirements of the Old Testament Law (as given to Moses in Exodus 20:1-17). If one should break The Law, he or she can now receive forgiveness. In the New Testament, Jesus summarized The Law and inscribes his Law of Love in our hearts.

Love the Lord your God with all your heart and with all your soul and with all your mind. This is the first and greatest command-ment. And the second is like it: Love your neighbor as yourself (Mat-thew 22:37-39).

The law, though, still plays a role in the life of a Believer—not as a measure of salvation but as a moral and ethical guide obeyed out of love for God, and by the power the Spirit provides (Romans 8:4-5 and footnote).

Those who live in accordance with the Spirit have their minds set on what the Spirit desires (Romans 8:5). Those who are led by the Spirit of God are Sons of God (Romans 8:14). When we listen and follow the Spirit we are heirs of God and co-heirs with Christ, we share in his suffering, so we may share in his glory (Romans 8:15 -17).

It is not through our own goodness that we receive these rights and privileges. It is by grace that *we are saved, through faith - it is a gift of God - not of works lest any man should boast* (Ephesians 2:8-10).

Jesus turned the Old Testament Law into a Covenant of Love and wrote his love upon our hearts. We obey now not out of obedience to fulfill the requirements of The Law, but because of his love written upon our hearts. Jesus set us free under this new covenant. Jesus loves us unconditionally, freeing us to choose to love others unconditionally.

CHOOSE LOVE

Everyone has a freewill. The gift of freedom God grants mankind is nothing less than the freedom to choose. You are not to give up your freewill, nor lay it at the feet of another. Each one of us is accountable before God for the choices we make. You are using your freewill wisely when you make the Kingdom choice to love others. The following examples clarify how you can choose to love in all circumstances.

Love is a choice. You choose how you will act and how you will respond. Once you secure that Kingdom choice, your feelings follow. Jesus chooses to love us unconditionally, so we are free to choose to love others unconditionally. Jesus' covenant with us is one of love (John 15:9-12). Love is the *Heartbeat* of the Kingdom.

You do not love sin but you love people, separating the sin from the person so you can love without condition. When you choose to love, Jesus' supernatural love flows through you. When you cannot love, Jesus' supernatural love will flow through you and change you.

LOVE is patient, LOVE is kind,

It does not envy,
It does not boast,
It is not proud.
It is not rude,

It is not self-seeking,
It is not easily angered,
It keeps no record of wrongs.

LOVE does not delight in evil but rejoices with the truth.

It always protects,
Always trusts,
Always hopes,
Always perseveres.
Love never fails!
1 Corinthians 13:1-7

LOVE NEVER FAILS

Everyone has feelings. Feelings are neither right nor wrong. Feelings are temporary and can be fragile, changing from moment to moment, even deceiving us at times. Feelings differ from love because love does not depend upon feelings. Love is a choice you make with your eyes wide open. You can rule over your emotions.

Sometimes you can feel as if you are not in love, or no longer can love, because you have been hurt. Your emotions and feelings, however, will follow the choices you make. You can, for instance, choose love. In choosing love you choose to forgive, choose to be healed and choose to bless - feelings should not rule over these choices. When you rule over your emotions, the power of the Kingdom can be released to others. Since God's Kingdom is the Kingdom of love, when you choose love you connect with the power that sets people free.

You are not to totally ignore feelings for they can warn of danger, be a checkpoint in relationships or a reminder to take care of your physical body. But, you do not depend upon feelings for your relationship with God or with others. Check your feelings to see if they agree with the Word of God. If not, change them so they do.

HOW TO CHOOSE LOVE WHEN YOU HAVE BEEN HURT

There are both intentional and unintentional hurts, hurts that cause us to withdraw our love and become protective, angry, bitter, hateful or full of revenge. The reason for our hurt is not as important as how we *respond* to our hurt. If we have been hurt or feel we can no longer love others, we need to stand and forgive. There are three steps to restoring a love relationship, three steps in the forgiveness process.

THE FIRST STEP IN FORGIVENESS

The first step in restoring a relationship is simple but profound: we must chose to forgive, as God commands (Colossians 3:12-14). When we stand to pray, forgive (Mark 11:25-26). We forgive so our sins might be forgiven, as Jesus taught us in the Lord's Prayer (Matthew 6:12-15). We forgive to release others and ourselves from darkness (John 20:23). We forgive because the Lord forgave - and forgives - us. We forgive because God forgives those we forgive.

Forgiveness releases both the one forgiven and the one who needs forgiveness. Jesus set the greatest example when he spoke from the cross, *"Father forgive them, for they know not what they do"* (Luke 23:34).

Lack of forgiveness imprisons others and us. If we stand in judgment and do not forgive, we not only bind those who offended us, we also end up imprisoning ourselves in darkness. (Matthew 18:21-35).

Forgiveness is not an easy choice, but it is the only Kingdom choice. Sometimes we do not feel like forgiving, but since forgiveness is a choice of our will, we choose forgiveness rather than how we feel. Our feelings will follow our choice. We continue to choose until we own that choice.

You can always forgive but that does not necessarily mean you should always trust. If you are in a situation where you or your children are being physically abused, forgive but do not allow yourself to continue to stay in the situation where abuse is happening. God will make a way out of this type of situation. Ask and he will direct you.

THE SECOND STEP IN FORGIVENESS

The second step is to release the hurt. So often, this second part of forgiveness is completely forgotten and the hurt continues to seethe, surfacing again in actions or reactions. When walls within prevent us from loving again, it may be because hurts have not been completely released. Release your hurt, determining that it will not rule over you or your relationship(s). Ask Jesus to heal your hurt completely, allow him to heal. Ask him for healing. Healing can be instantaneous or take place over an extended time. Continue to strike the ground until healing is complete.

As people under the Covenant of Love, we must settle the question in our hearts once and for all, our choice is *love.* To choose to love does not mean to trust. Know the heart condition of others and realize some people are not yet ready for complete trust.

THE THIRD STEP IN FORGIVENESS

Finally, we bless those who have spitefully used us - Christians and non-Christians. Non-Christians do not know God and really need forgiveness - God's and ours. (Romans 12:14, Matthew 5:43-48). When they come against us they have touched the apple of God's eye. When thinking of them, bless them in their job, bless their children, bless their home, bless them in any and every way possible - until the hurt has been forgotten. Blessing can also be an action, as well as a prayer; bless these people with an act of kindness.

Think of your children, (even the errant ones) as well as spouses or relatives, and others, praying blessings into their lives. As long as you feel negative pray blessings on them.

God wants you to learn and grow even if your hurt is not healed immediately. Continue to forgive, asking for healing and blessing every time the painful memory returns. Do this until the memory no longer hurts - not one minute longer, not one minute shorter. Keep striking that ground until you own it and you are free of the negative feelings.

Once, I prayed for three years over a particular reoccurring unpleasant memory. I do not know why it took so long (while other memories had been eliminated reasonably quick), but I knew the process and I persevered.

We cannot skip any steps in this process: forgiving, healing and blessing.

FORGIVENESS PRAYER: In the name of Jesus, I choose to love_____ (name of person). I stand and forgive this person for _____(offense). I thank God that he will touch and heal all the hurt I have received from this person. I ask God to touch and heal them. I pray God will pour out a great blessing on them in the following ways: _____, _____, and _____ Amen.

WHEN YOU NEED TO BE FORGIVEN

Actively seek forgiveness if you were/are at fault, not allowing pride to prevent the restoration of the relationship. Go to the person you have wronged and talk to them. Do not let them avoid the issue by saying, "That's OK." It is not OK to hurt others.

If you have approached the person you wronged with humility and sincerely offered apologies - yet they refuse to forgive you - forgive them, pray for their healing, and bless them. Very painful offenses may require a period of time for restoration to occur; a trust relationship may never be the same and a very precious friendship may be lost forever through carelessness. But be encouraged, as working through hurts sometimes binds people closer than they were before.

BE PREPARED

Relationships can be very difficult and can include intense feelings of anger. You may feel angry when someone is completely insensitive or invades your personal "space." Anger should not be stuffed inside and ignored. (This kind of response can cause severe depression.) Anger should be confronted and resolved. When you express anger, you should not display your temper in harmful ways. Shouting, name-calling or dragging up issues from the past only makes the problem more difficult to resolve. When dealing with anger, it is helpful to set some ground rules for yourself *before* problems surface. Think through how you handle anger - your own anger, as well as that of others - so you are ready to respond in a God-honoring way.

Anger must be faced and the problems solved so anger does not control us. Choose to love others and work out the problems so sin and lack of forgiveness can be avoided. Another reaction to anger is to choose not to be angry.

WISDOM IN FORGIVENESS

Forgiveness does not automatically produce miraculous, instantaneous change. The forgiven person can still hold grudges or be under spiritual bondage. Listen for the still, quiet voice of the Holy Spirit for direction as to when to return to the relationship.

When my foster daughter prayed forgiveness for her sexually abusive father, I cautioned her that although she had forgiven him that did not mean her relationship with her father was instantly or completely healed. She needed to wait for a strong confirmation of change. She did not heed my warning and that evening she ran back into the arms of an unchanged, sexually-abusive father. We must be obedient and forgive. As with every prayer and every direction, however, we wait upon the leading of the Lord to know how, when, or if the relationship is to be restored.

Sometimes we do not realize the need for forgiveness until an unpleasant memory roars unexpectedly to the surface. The memory could even be a non-verbal action such as withdrawal of affection or support at a particular time of great need. The person who acted in this matter can be totally unaware of the harm they have caused.

It is not necessary to point out every hurtful memory to others or every time you forgive. Those who must constantly remind others they are forgiving them are just stroking their own pride and not really into forgiving. Just forgive every time the memory is brought to mind, continuing to forgive, bless and pray to be healed until the pain is gone and the recall of the memory no longer causes pain. *Three important elements of forgiveness are:*

(1) Hurt is not always one-sided even though from your perspective it may appear one-sided. Two people can see the hurt from different perspectives; It is easy to focus on self and misread others' intentions.

(2) Be aware your heart may hide hurt and the need for forgiveness. Ask God to reveal hidden areas in your heart of any hurt or unforgiveness.

(3) We always need to accept full responsibility for all of our actions. We are not to blame others or excuse ourselves for sinning due to past hurt.

TYPES OF WAYS TO FORGIVE BROTHER TO BROTHER

When others have offended you, do not talk behind their back. Go to them and kindly let them know how you feel. This may be received several ways: they can respond by asking forgiveness in harming you, they may respond by not asking forgiveness, they may attempt to justify their actions, or they may refuse to hear of their wrongdoing.

THE MANIPULATOR

Once I went to a Christian neighbor to resolve a problem between our families. He was a manipulator, certain there was only one point of view - his! Because he would not admit fault or accept responsibility, he believed forgiveness and change between our families would only come if we submitted to his power and control. He also became verbally aggressive and abusive as we talked.

Forgive this type of behavior and bind the person's judgments away from you and your family. Trust God to deal with them. Do not try to please them (they can not hear correction or words of reason). Do not involve yourself with them nor try to reason with them.

Sometimes they are not as obvious as this man was, but watch and keep away from people who try to control you. If you must resolve the problem, return with two or three others (Matthew 18:15-16). Never work with this type of person alone.

There is another kind of manipulator whose actions are more skillful. This person is outwardly loving and kind. They shrewdly allow you to know of their needs so you, as a good Christian, can meet those needs. They use you because of your generous and giving nature, or because they recognize you have an emotional need they can exploit.

Their actions may appear to be gracious, but they are self-serving. Their actions also contradict their words. If you should become suspicious they often loudly claim offense, covering their actions with good-sounding excuses to make you appear the villain. They play on emotions and, if their needs are not met, they move on to prey elsewhere.

When we love with Kingdom covenant love it is a strong love. We love unconditionally but we do not allow our love, feelings, or choices to be manipulated.

RECONCILIATION

Reconciliation can be the answer to some relationship problems. God offers His people the ministry of reconciliation (2 Corinthians 5:17-20). Reconciliation can happen with or without the actual confronting of hurts. Sometimes the parties involved need to discuss the actual event and ask for forgiveness, but there are times when such a discussion would make resolving differences more difficult. Perhaps the two parties are coming from two different perspectives. In this situation it is not who is right, but can you agree to love and not allow your differences or misunderstandings to separate you. Can you choose to allow love to be the basis for your relationship?

Sometimes people want to justify their position, making it more difficult for actual reconciliation to take place. Therefore, there are times when saying nothing but, "Let's be reconciled," is best. Sometimes, perhaps because of pride, immaturity, or spiritual bondage, a person is unable to admit fault even though they know they are wrong. We can still put on the ministry of reconciliation and stand for love in that relationship. Whichever way God directs you to reconcile is the way you reconcile.

Once God told me to reconcile because the other person was not able to say they were sorry. This person wept publicly after being approached and simply asked, "Can we reconcile?" Two months later that person became Spirit-filled. As we forgive, we release people to God.

It is important to wait upon God's timing in these situations. I waited six months, but I did not move back into the relationship until prompted to do so by the Holy Spirit. The Spirit is faithful to prompt us to move when the time is ready. We obey and everything falls into place. There was a struggle as I waited though. I looked and searched diligently for what God would have me do.

Faithfully look for your answer and you will recognize it when it comes.

WHEN YOU HAVE DONE ALL - STAND

Many years ago, I heard someone share a vision that emphasized the importance of standing in the right place at the right time. In their vision they observed a large crowd of people streaming up the pathway to the top of a mountain. They saw themselves blend into and become a part of the crowd as it moved towards the top of the mountain. As the crowd reached the top before them spread an open pathway that led to the edge of a sheer cliff. On the edge of the cliff stood other Christians forming a human barrier to prevent those in the throng from simply falling over the ledge.

The person saw a place on the edge of the cliff designated for them. They made their way through the throng and joined the Christians on the brink of the mountain cliff as part of the human barrier. But there were places on the edge of the cliff where no one stood. In those places people poured through the gaps, careening over the sheer bluff.

This vision aptly describes how, as part of the body of Christ, we each have a definite place to stand. In standing we form a human barrier to prevent those who are not Christians, (and those who are Christians but have lost their way) from falling off their cliff.

The Word states that when you have done all else, stand (Ephesians 6:11-17). To stand means to stay where you are and pray for another. It means to stand, immovable in prayer, until you have the answer for that person or it can be just simply not moving until the Spirit directs you to move. For example: moving out of a ministry or leaving a church body or a friendship. It can mean that just your physical presence is part of your prayer.

There are times to stand silently in prayer, never allowing another to know you are praying. You can pray forgiveness where they are not praying for themselves or do not see the need to pray. Forgive hurt inflicted on you or on others. Pray until you and others are healed. Also, actively bless them and demand that any evil spirits involved, be bound. Stand praying, loving unconditionally and interceding for them before God. You are standing and preventing them from falling over the edge of that cliff. You guard and pray carefully for this person may be in such a battle or emotional turmoil, approaching them openly to discuss any issues would only stir up animosity between the two of you. Love unconditionally and leave the rest to Jesus. This is a quiet, yet active, stand in prayer.

There are times to stand in the midst of a problem in order to view the problem clearly so you can determine where and how to pray. If you leave the situation too quickly you will not recognize where prayer is needed. God often calls his people to stand in difficult places "until further notice." God teaches us valuable lessons as we follow his purpose and voice, waiting for the Spirit to confirm the time to move on (Proverbs 16:3).

Sometimes, after you have stood in prayer or in a position for a season, God urges you to move physically away from the people you have been near or for whom you have prayed. Perhaps God called you to intercede, but he lets you know when a job is finished.

Once I stood in prayer for a ministry, even becoming part of that ministry. I had to stand there to see the need for prayer. After about three months, to my complete surprise, I knew the time was over. Knowing this I did not move, but continued to physically stand in prayer two more months waiting confirmation. One evening, some friends came to visit. As they left the husband turned to me and completely out of context stated vehemently, "It is time for you to return to where you were!" It was as if someone physically kicked a stool out from under my feet. I knew my "stand" was gone and I was free to leave. I let the church I was attending know God was moving me on and I returned to where I belonged. I was only there briefly to help pray for the needs of the church.

If you attend and support a ministry you need *to stand* with that ministry in positive prayer. Every ministry will have its problems, just because people are people. Whatever ministry you are a part of, you share your anointing - the gifting the Holy Spirit has given you - with them. You are to be there and share until the Holy Spirit moves you on. But do not continue to lend your anointing once the Spirit has directed you to move on. Sometimes you move where God needs you, sometimes the Spirit moves you out of a ministry for reasons you do not fully understand until later.

In I Samuel 15:10-26, King Saul lied to the prophet Samuel

and disobeyed the Lord. Saul passed the blame onto others for his disobedience. The prophet Samuel, who previously had supported Saul, laid bare Saul's disobedience. At that point the prophet could no longer stand with Saul nor support Saul with his prophetic gifts.

LOVING, FORGIVING AND BLESSING YOUR OWN FLESH
THE MARRIAGE COVENANT

A Christian marriage is a blood covenant between male and female, a covenant blessed and established by God himself. A man and a woman become one flesh when they marry (Genesis 2:23-25) and that which affects one also affects the other. In establishing a Kingdom relationship, man and woman walk beside each other as one flesh. The woman is the man's partner - she is not underneath the man. Being underneath the man is being under the curse (Genesis 3:16).

All the prayers you pray for yourself can be prayed and claimed for your mate and your children. You can pray forgiveness, pray for their hearts to be changed and pray that their hurts will be healed.

The husband covers and protects his wife in prayer. Together, husband and wife should pray for the blessing and protection of their children, relatives, work situations and common needs. Together their prayers are stronger than when they pray alone. In prayer they should share their deepest needs with each other rather than with friends.

Be careful in conversations concerning your mate. It is good to gain wise counsel from those with godly wisdom, but be prudent and watchful with your words. Some people, frankly, are not worthy of personal trust.

Because you are one flesh with your mate, do not pray judgment upon them - your problems will only increase. The Kingdom we belong to is an unseen one and we must believe God and his blessings more than that which we see with our own eyes. If we pray blessing we also receive it - another excellent reason to pray blessing.

This does not mean ignoring mistakes and faults; do not ignore reality but pray *knowing* reality. You will be hurt by your spouse, but, you must choose to forgive, bless and struggle to be healed. This is a strong kind of love. This is Kingdom love, the kind of love that changes lives.

CHILDREN

A pattern of constant, negative thoughts or statements from parents to their children has far-reaching affects, and can act like curses. Negative thinking about your children can work like negative prayers. Children need to be released into the hands of their heavenly Father. They are, after all, his children first. He will covenant with us for our children.

Love always hopes, always perseveres. Love prays the answers - not the problems.

PRAYER: I CHOOSE to pray blessing on_____(name of children or spouse). I ask forgiveness for their rebellion, and in Jesus name, I pray for a healing of their hearts. Amen.

"My Spirit, who is on you, and my words that I have put in your mouth, will not depart from your mouth, or from the mouths of your children, or from the mouths of their descendants from this time on and forever," says the Lord (Isaiah 59:21).

FORGIVING OURSELVES

All have sinned and fall short of the glory of God (Romans 3:23). However, *there is no condemnation for those who are in Christ Jesus* (Romans 8:1).

Because God completely forgives us, who are we not to forgive ourselves? When we feel convicted of sin, we need to seek forgiveness for ourselves and seek forgiveness from others. In prayer we seek forgiveness by confessing sin, thereby reconciling ourselves to God. If we still feel the guilt we may need to confess the sin to another (James 5:16).

Sometimes guilt lifts with an open confession - a very powerful kind of confession. As long as sin hides within, the enemy is allowed to torment. Once it is out in the open, the enemy loses his power to use guilt against us.

When we feel conviction, we need to repent. Condemnation, however, is not from God. When we condemn ourselves or others condemn us, we feel a great weight of guilt. Our eyes are focused upon self and not on God. Condemnation becomes a point of self-centeredness, a destructive cycle. We have to forgive and let go, breaking the destructive cycle by accepting God's provision for forgiveness.

PRAYER: Lord forgive me for _____ (sin[s] committed). I repent of my actions and thank you for helping me destroy the influences of this sin on my life. Amen.

If the enemy of your soul returns to torment you with condemnation, return to this prayer and date it.

SOUL TIES

Soul ties are emotional connections that bind you to another person. You may not even realize they exist, but if you pray for release, God will grant it.

If you have been married more than once, you became one flesh with your previous spouse. If you entered into a sexual relationship outside your marriage, you became one flesh with that person. These *soul ties* must be cut and eliminated from a previous marriage(s) and/or the out-of-wedlock sin, through confession. This emotional bondage, left in place, will prevent the exercise of free will in Kingdom living.

These ties affect the mind, will and emotions. Whenever we enter into a personal relationship with another such as a parent, surrogate parent, relative, strong friend, cult leader or sexual partner, a strong emotional tie develops.

This emotional tie can cause a person to ignore their true, personal feelings or decisions in order to please, appease or receive acceptance from another. If you are in such a relationship, this sin needs to be confessed. If there has been victimization or overly strong emotional ties, these can be cut if one of the people involved is willing to pray.

Cutting these ties leaves a person free to make their own decisions without pressure and without their free will being violated. Soul ties need to be cut between parents and their parents, children and their parents, good friends, pastors, and any others the Holy Spirit brings to mind.

PRAYER: In the name of Jesus, I sever all emotional ties that hold me captive. Specifically, I sever that tie between myself and _____ (name of person[s]). I ask forgiveness for allowing this tie to compromise my relationship with you, Jesus. Thank you, Lord, for freeing me so I might follow only you and give complete allegiance of my heart to you. Amen.

JUDGMENTS

Do not judge, or you, too, will be judged. For in the same way you judge others you will be judged, and with the measure you use, it will be measured to you.   Matthew 7:1-2

Our judgmental words can bind others. When we judge others we must repent of our careless words and pray all negative judgments stop and their power be broken. Remember, there is only one Lawgiver, one judge (James 4:12). The words with which you judge others will come upon you (Matthew 7:1).

We have the key to both bind and loose others with our words, prayers or judgments. We want to bind what is not of God and loose into the lives of others what is of God.   (Matthew 16:19).

*I will give you the keys of the kingdom of heaven; Whatever you bind on earth will be bound in heaven; And whatever you loose on earth will be loosed in heaven. (*Matthew 16:19).

Christians and non-Christians alike can judge and bind us, casting doubt on our reputation. Their words have power and can cause confusion. A sense of heaviness and doubt, like a heavy cloud, can cover and oppress us, causing us to feel guilty - but not understand why. If you recognize these symptoms, pray that the power of their judgments would stop. You will feel a great heaviness lift, and such prayer is often followed by tremendous blessings (that were previously withheld because of judgments against you).

We are also capable of placing judgments upon ourselves. "I am sick and tired! Why am I so stupid? I'm just a loser! My mind will never understand!"

Our ears hear these things and the body responds to our

self-judgments. We need to repent and ask forgiveness for self-imposed curses. Pray that negative judgments will cease, and stop using negative language.

Your family or peers may have judged you, because judgments can follow through a generation or be continued through verbal abuse. Parents, peers or teachers may have planted curses into your mind and spirit when you were a young child. These negative worlds can continue to produce negative results. "You're worthless, a failure, no good, stupid," repeated over and over again, could result in your unwittingly accepting those judgments.

A teacher could have harmfully labeled you by repeatedly calling you a "slow learner!" You then file away these judgments in your memory, accepting them as truth until you pray and break this hold.

You can judge others: labeling them, judging their motives, decisions, commitment. Sometimes it is not *what* is said, but the inflection or tone of voice used. Learn to speak truth without using a judgmental tone.

As well as loosing yourself from judgment you also need to forgive those who have judged you. Whether you have given or accepted judgment, you need to pray:

PRAYERS: In the name of Jesus, I command any judgments coming to me from _____ (name of person[s]) to stop. These judgments are to be broken and no longer influence my life or the life of those in my family. I stand and freely forgive. Also, forgive me for all the judgments I have made against _____.(name of person[s] you have judged). I repent for judging them and now release them from all my judgments. God, I pray you will bless them. Amen.

When you choose to use the supernatural love of Jesus, practice forgiveness, use wisdom in relationships, bless your marriage partner and your children, loose judgments, and reconcile relationships, you beat the ground with zeal and defeat the wiles of the enemy. You truly are taking the Kingdom by force of love.

THE KING'S EDICT

*Bless those who curse you and pray for
those who spitefully use you.*

PART 2   BEAT THE GROUND WITH FAITH

God speaks and, by faith, we believe. We believe God is who he says he is, and will do what he says he will do...and so, in faith, we physically respond. As the writer of Hebrews says, *Without faith it is impossible to please God, because anyone who comes to him must believe that he exists, and that he rewards those who earnestly seek him (*Hebrews 11:6).

How then do we active faith? Faith is a choice - an action in word or deed. This action then makes substance of things that did not exist before. Faith is the substance maker of the Kingdom.

FAITH AS A CHOICE

Faith is a choice, just as love is a choice. You can choose to believe God and act on that choice, believe in that choice, and set your course by that choice. The choice to believe or act should not be determined by feelings or circumstances. The great Patriarch of the Old Testament, Abraham, is an excellent life to examine. Abraham is considered the father of faith because he believed God.

Abraham believed God and it was credited to him as righteousness (Romans 4:3b). It was not through the law that Abraham and his offspring received the promise that he would be heir of the world, but through the righteousness that comes by faith (Romans 4:13).

Abraham and his offspring received the promise because of faith. So when you choose faith you win ground for yourselves and for your children. But what if you don't feel as if you believe?

Feelings are not necessarily important in the faith factor. Feelings can be fickle. Sometimes feelings can rise in great emotional fever and then one is ready to believe. If God speaks a *rhema* word to us and our feelings are not stimulated, respond based on God - not your feelings. Feelings should follow your choices. If you choose to believe God, feelings align with your choices *as you believe.*

You can experience doubt and still have faith. Doubt is a feeling and feelings come and go. They are neither right or wrong. Only as you act on the wrong feeling are actions wrong. You express faith as you act upon the Word. Doubt can be a reason to confirm again our pathway before God. Abraham, for example, had some anxious moments, but God did not count them against him (Romans 4:19 and footnote). You can have anxious moments and God will not hold them against you.

Circumstances can be deceptive and should not determine our faith. It can appear as if you are on the wrong road heading away from the prize of the Kingdom goal. True, you might have chosen differently, but God is in control. He knows the path we need to travel. Recognize it is God, not circumstances that determine your destiny. God uses circumstances to teach you and that path can include suffering. But through that suffering he will teach you victory.

You possess the Kingdom through the physical action of making your feelings follow your choices and by knowing God is in charge all of your circumstances. You exercise faith when you respond to a *rhema* word God has dropped into your heart or placed into practice through biblical principals.

God works through a *rhema* words. As God drops this *rhema* word into your heart and you respond, the Holy Spirit will continue to clarify your direction. Take, for example, Noah and the ark (Genesis 6:11-9:1). Noah had a rhema word from God, "Build an ark!" This sheepherder responded and built an ark on dry land. Noah was not a boat builder, he was a sheepherder. He became a boat builder in response to God's rhema word. When he rode in the ark above the waters, he was a sheepherder that had built a boat. Due to his obedience, when his ark of faith landed, he literally owned the whole world. If we follow in obedience and build our ark of faith, we will literally own the world when it lands.

God also works through Kingdom Principles clearly defined in Scripture. When one chooses to apply these principles, they are beating the ground for the Kingdom to be established on earth as it is in heaven.

The following are some Kingdom principles to respond to with physical acts or actions. (You have an advocate with the Father, so when you make mistakes you can ask forgiveness and begin again.) The principles do not include the *rhema* word of God, because each of us can receive different *rhema* words from God. The principles listed are: Seek First the Kingdom, The Sabbath Rest, Power of our Words, Speaking to a Circumstance, Stewardship, Tithing, Reaping and Sowing, Discipleship, Submission, Unity, and Honor. There are assuredly more principles, however, as you begin, take *careful* note - principles are not to be valued above relationship! Principles are simply outward actions performed out of love for the relationship, not to manipulate. The relationship is always the priority! The reason you are privy to the relationship, Kingdom living, and Kingdom success is only because of the blood sacrifice of Jesus. You are just an imperfect, saved person on your Kingdom journey learning Kindgom principles.

SEEK FIRST THE KINGDOM

Seek first his kingdom and his righteousness, and all these things will be given to you as well. Matthew 6:33

We are not to worry about what we will eat, drink or what clothes we will wear, for as you seek the Kingdom and God's righteousness, all these things will follow. *But first* seek the Kingdom! In seeking first God's Kingdom, you must set aside all other kingdoms.

THE SABBATH REST

There remains, then, a Sabbath-rest for the people of God; for anyone who enters God's rest also rests from his own work, just as God did from his (Hebrews 4:9-10).

The people Moses led out of the bondage of Egypt were not able to enter God's rest, the Promised Land, because of their unbelief and the hardness of their hearts. They wandered in the desert forty years until all those who did not believe died (Deuteronomy 1:26-36).

When the last of this unbelieving generation died, Joshua delivered the new generation (those who believed God) into the

Promised Land. Joshua was convinced of the power of God's promises to overcome the circumstances of giants and other difficulties confronting him. He had the faith to believe when God said, *"Only be strong and courageous and every place where you tread I will give to you (Joshua 1:1-9)."*

You, too, have been delivered out of bondage. *Today if you hear his voice harden not your hearts* (Hebrews 4:7). As with Joshua, only be strong and courageous and every place upon which you tread God will give to you.

Believe that God is, and that he rewards those who diligently seek him, and, no matter what the circumstances, choose to believe God. In choosing to believe God you activate faith and enter into the promised rest, a rest without condemnation.

POWER OF OUR WORDS

A wise man's heart guides his mouth. Proverbs 16:23

In our tongue is the power of life and death. Be careful not to pattern your speech after the speech of the world (Proverbs 18:20,21; Numbers 14:26-29; Matthew 12:35-37).

With our tongues we can commit to bless people, not curse them. If I am driving in my car and someone cuts in front of me and I choose to swear at them I am cursing them by the power of my negative words. We are all made in God's image and we are not to curse that image (Genesis 1:26; James 3:9, Genesis 9:6 see footnote). Put away perversity from your mouth (Proverbs 4:24).

If you speak behind someone's back, even if your sentences sound harmless, these careless words are bringing judgments, and the person stands judged by your words. If you have something to say you should say it with kindness and honesty, directly to them. They then have the opportunity to respond to your words. Walk very carefully here though. Not everything needs to be to spoken. Honesty should not and is not an excuse to abuse verbally; it must be balanced with love and wisdom. Often things need to be just let go in love.

Do everything without complaining or arguing, so that you may be come blameless and pure, children of God without fault in a crooked and depraved generation, in which you shine like stars in the universe as you hold out the Word of life. (Philippians 2:14).

Those using Kingdom words do not seek to build self-esteem or self-reliance, that is a building up of your kingdom of self. God's perspective is to speak his plan into the lives of others until it is revealed and believed, having faith on their behalf. These are not empty words but creative words of faith in action. Because God has called his people from the womb for a purpose and a destiny, we simply agree with God and his perspective. And then invest ourselves in that perspective. When God has given you a promise, instead of saying, "It will never happen," agree with God about what he is going to do, speaking the promise back to God - in faith. God, hearing your belief, will respond.

Using the tongue's creative power does not mean just to be a positive speaker in order to manipulate others or God, but it means agreeing with God and his perfect purpose.

SPEAKING TO A CIRCUMSTANCE

If circumstances feel overpowering, we have the authority to command them to come under our feet. Everything is under the feet of Jesus and, as co-heirs with Jesus, we have that same authority (Ephesians 1:20-23, Romans 8:17).

Focus on Jesus instead of on the circumstance. You can do this by commanding everything to come under your feet. You pray, insisting the circumstances move, until you sense you are walking above the circumstances. The circumstances may not have changed but you are now standing with a different perspective. They are under your feet, not hovering over your head.

Peter walked above his circumstances when he walked on the water to Jesus. As long as Peter kept his eyes on the Master, he never sank. However, as soon as he looked away, his circumstances began to overwhelm him. It is only as we turn our eyes to Jesus that we will be rescued (Matthew 14:25-31).

STEWARDSHIP

More is given to those who are good stewards, because they know it belongs to the Kingdom and is only on loan to them. It is loaned so that it can be shared with those in need. Kingdom wealth is entrusted to those who will use it for Kingdom purposes. If you see a brother without a coat, give him one of yours (Matthew 5:40-48, Matthew 6:1-4). Be a good steward over all God gives to you.

TITHING

Giving to the Lord of your income is not simply for the purpose of multiplying your money but for taking of physical control of your funds. It is a statement of faith to take your funds and place them under God's authority (2 Corinthians 9:6-8). It is a physical action taking funds out of the kingdom of this world and placing them into the Kingdom of God.

Kingdom monetary rules: (Malachi 3:6-12)

- God REBUKES the devourer.
- God MULTIPLIES resources to his people.
- God MEETS our needs.

When a person chooses to tithe of their income, they place their money into the Kingdom under Kingdom supervision where it is carefully guarded.

REAPING AND SOWING

For every Kingdom action there is a reaction. Whatever you are planting into your life or the lives of others - whether it is faith, the Word of God, forgiveness, charity, or finances - you will receive back. Sow generously into the Kingdom and you will reap generously (2 Corinthians 9:6-8).

The opposite is also true: The negative things you plant into your life will yield an infected crop. If you have been sowing negatively, repent, and turn. For a while you may still reap from negative seeding.

If, for example, you have been a thief but have decided to stop stealing, you may have to pay through the criminal courts for your actions.

DISCIPLESHIP

Salvation is a free gift, but if you want to be a disciple you pay a price. The price is letting go of your own will and way. The free grace Jesus offers cost him everything. If you take that sacrifice lightly and go about your own business, you then, are not a true disciple (Luke 14:25-28).

HONOR, SUBMISSION AND UNITY

Give honor to whom those who honor is due. The first to honor is your parents. This is the only commandment with a promise: *Honor your father and your mother so that you may live long in the land the Lord is giving you.* To honor is to respect, esteem, and to make your parents proud by the way you live your life (Exodus 20:12).

Submit to the Lord your God and follow him with all your heart. If you are married, your spouse will be sanctified by your choice (1 Corinthians 7:14). Jesus gave his life so that what Adam lost in the Garden of Eden would be restored - man and woman walking together as one. Live in unity, for where there is unity, God bestows his blessing (Psalm 133:1-3, Romans 15:5-6).

ACCOUNTABILITY

Wives are to be accountable and faithful to their husbands. Husbands are to be accountable and faithful to their wives. Children are to be accountable to their parents. Pastors are to be accountable to God for the people God gives into their care. (Proverbs 31:10-33, 20:6; Ephesians 5:22-25, 6:1-3, 4:11-13).

If you are a disciple, a representative of Jesus, know that disciples are faithful at their place of work, and they cheerfully pay bills and taxes on time. And remember, those things come with practice. God just appreciates it when we practice. He is not looking for perfection but someone who has a willing heart to learn.

Disciples are people of the Word. They are to be accountable and faithful to perform their words and promises in a timely fashion and not to speak careless, empty words. The world is watching to see if Christians speak empty words or if they are really doers of their words and doers of the words of God.

FAITH AS AN ATTITUDE

Faith is an attitude of gratitude, thanksgiving and praise toward God. The Word of God repeatedly admonishes and encourages us to have that right attitude, praising God in all things. We can praise God through music, verbal words of praise and thanksgiving, and worship. We praise because:

We know that all things work for the good of those who love the Lord. Romans 8:28

MUSIC

Music can bypass the mind and move uncensored into the soul. Music touches your emotions as little else can and is, therefore a powerful force.

According to Bernice Regan Johnson, music can have a positive influence on the air through which it travels, and upon those the air touches. In her interview program aired on Public Broadcasting System, "The Songs are Free," Mrs. Johnson relates how during the 60's gospel music was a major factor in easing racial tensions. Police, tenement owners and shop owners witnessed freedom rallies attended by blacks, where the air felt thick and oppressive. If someone started an old gospel hymn, however, voices would quickly be raised in unison and praise. The song would fill the air, nullifying the intense anger.

Praise music can be used as tool. You reclaim the Kingdom by praising the name of Jesus. Praise pulls down the strongholds of the enemy.

PRAISE

We praise because of who God is and who God is to us, not to manipulate. Praising to receive only what you want is manipulation and God will not be tricked. If you use words of praise simply as words of conversation, they become ineffective as either praise or conversation.

Because a grateful heart moves the hand of God and brings good out of all bad situations, this Kingdom principle activates the miraculous. You have relationship with God, and although evil surrounds you, it will be used for your good. We do not operate on the same level as the world, but upon Kingdom principles. God is God and he can bring about good whether you praise him or not. He brings about good and, therefore, you can praise him.

Praise breaks the hold of the enemy. The enemy cannot stand praise! He will vacate the space in order to be away from praise. Therefore we are to praise not considering circumstances but give a sacrifice of praise through our difficult times, lifting up the name of Jesus.

Sometimes, especially when we are complaining and whining, we need an attitude adjustment. Because praise is a choice - an attitude of gratitude - when you choose to praise, your attitude will change. Praise God for that! Who likes a stinky attitude? Not God!

WORSHIP

Worship occurs as you enter into a higher place of praise.

Worship leads us into a very holy place, the throne room of God, his very presence. These are some of the different kinds of praise: sacrificial praise, praising God because he is good, praising just because God is who he says he is and is our all in all, praising out of gratitude, and praising to enter into God's presence.

MUSIC, PRAISE, AND WORSHIP are power-packed gifts for bringing our petitions and needs before God, power-packed ways to tear down the strongholds of Satan, the prince of the air. As the air around us is filled with praise, music and worship, it affects the air and the people breathing that air.

The enemy cannot stand the praises of God and will flee from where praise and worship are being offered. I have seen the enemy fall as praise was offered. I have witnessed miracles as I praised God in difficult circumstances, sometimes even through tears. The biggest miracle of all is the changes he accomplishes in my heart.

Suffering is real and there will be times and seasons to praise through suffering. But, there is a need to know and practice spiritual warfare so that you do not praise God for unnecessary suffering.

THE SERVANT

You not only have an attitude of gratitude, your attitude is to be that of a servant. You are called to serve.

You know that the rulers of the Gentiles lord it over them, and their high officials exercise authority over them. Not so with you!
Instead, whoever wants to become great among you must be your servant, a*nd who ever wants to be first must be your slave. Just as the Son of Man did not come to be served, but to serve, and to give his life as a ransom for many.* Matthew 20:25-28

You are to worship the Lord your God, and him alone (Matthew 4:10), serving him with your whole heart. Jesus submitted his own will, even unto death, to serve at the Father's command. Jesus was the perfect example of a servant King. In serving God you wait upon him, prepare your hearts for him and allow him the opportunity to speak and direct your life. One service you are to offer is to serve one another in love (Galatians 5:13).

However you are to serve only when and where God calls. If you serve when you are not called, you serve only self. This type of *service* does not please God. Therefore we are not to take upon ourselves things to do because simply because someone else says that we are suppose to do them, or because of our area of gifting. In all areas we are to wait upon the Lord and lend our ear to the direction he has for our life. We become a servant of the Lord not a servant to man. We become a servant to the Lord not a servant to self. In becoming a servant of the Lord we walk as his Kingdom people.

FAITH AS SUBSTANCE

Faith comes by hearing and hearing by the Word of God. Faith is the evidence of things not yet seen. When one has faith or belief that God will do what he has promised, a deposit (literally) is made into their account in the Kingdom. Now those of faith, and their offspring, can draw on this account (Romans 4:3, 4:13).

Abraham exhibited faith and God counted it to him as righteousness. What is true for Abraham is true for us also (Romans 4:23-24, Romans 4:16 see footnotes). God will credit faith as righteousness to us and to our children as we believe in him and act on that belief.

PART 3   BEAT THE GROUND WITH HOPE

Hope is a place, a relationship and a future. If you place your hope in the things of this world or yourself, instead of Christ, you can lose hope very quickly. To lose hope is to live in a place of devastation, left with nothing to live for, utterly hopeless. Hope is keeping your eyes on the one who gives out hope.

You have hope that you will become all God has called you to be. You can have hope in God, as God honors those who serve him, and God rewards those who earnestly seek him (Hebrews 11:6). You hope for yourself as you place your hope in Christ and find in him an anchor of safety for it is safe to hope in Jesus. In him you can find a relationship and a destiny. God will never forget us, as he has carved us on the palm of his hands (Isaiah 49:15-16). Within the relationship there is stability and security for every son God accepts, he disciplines (keeps in line) for their own safety (Hebrews 12:5-11). He is in this for the long term and he builds character in us through suffering and perseverance.

God builds character and hope into his citizens. Suffering produces perseverance, perseverance produces character and character produces hope (Romans 5:3-5).

INTERCESSION

You can hope for family, friends, strangers or for your city, country, and leaders, interceding for them in prayer. When others have no hope, you commit to hope for them as you stand faithfully before God in prayer for their future.

Intercession is repenting for the sins of others, asking forgiveness and healing for the sins of others, and standing in the place of prayer for them if they do not, or cannot, pray. You can also hope for them through the Isaiah 58 fast or physical fasting. When you practice hope for them you beat the ground for them where they did not have the strength for themselves. So you beat the ground with great zeal until the snakes leave and the one you have held out hope for finally can see the Kingdom of God.

This is not typical prayer it involves a struggle. Pray, praise and quote the Word. Be led by the Spirit. If you choose to intercede or pray specifically by wrestling in prayer, first, make sure your heart is clean before God. Be attentive in listening to direction and discernment from the Holy Spirit.

*Note: *Every prayer within this text can be used as intercessory prayer for spouses, children and parents.*

FASTING

The kind of fast the Lord requires of us is to first have charity, love, and consideration for others. Fasting without charity is only an outward action, producing nothing of lasting value. There are several different ways to fast. Consider the Isaiah 58 Fast as one that offers great blessing and a fast that God himself recommends.

THE ISAIAH 58 FAST

Is not this the kind of fasting I have chosen: to loose the chains of injustice, untie the cords of the yoke, to set the oppressed free and break every yoke?

Is it not to share your food with the hungry? Provide the poor wanderer with shelter? When you see the naked, to clothe him? And do not turn away from your own flesh and blood.

Then your light will break forth like the dawn, and your healing will quickly appear; and your righteousness will go before you, and the Glory of the Lord will be your rear guard.

Then you call, and the Lord will answer; You will cry for help, and the Lord will say: "Here I am." Isaiah 58:6-9

Therein lies the true fast, one that is born out of love and sacrifice. There are also physical fasts. They can include certain parts of a day or week, whole days, certain foods.

A fast can be in response to a call from the Holy Spirit, for the nation, others or for yourself. Fasting is a matter of continually choosing to be obedient. As with any type of personal denial, you need to be aware of your own limitations. A diabetic individual, for example, should not skip meals.

When one fasts it is not to be done publicly, but, quietly and unto the Lord (Matthew 6:16-18). Jesus puts food into perspective when he says, *"My food is to do the will of him who sent me and to finish his work"* (John 4:34).

HOPE FOR OUR NATION

You can hope for your nation. You hope by praying and fasting and turning from your sin. Praying and repenting personally for the forgiveness of the sin of your city, your nation. God promises to hear these prayers and heal your land.

The healing of the land is not dependent upon those in the world, those who do not know Jesus. The healing of the land is dependent upon followers of Jesus like you and me - and our prayers before God. We are the ones responsible for the state of the nation because we have not stood in prayer, in faith, and repentance.

If My People will humble themselves and pray, seek my face and turn from their wicked ways, then will I hear from heaven, forgive their sin and heal their land (2 Chronicles 7:14).

SIGNS AND WONDERS, THE FAVOR OF GOD, AND PROPHECY

Signs and Wonders accompany the Believer, therefore as a Believer you can expect them to follow you. (Mark 16:17). You can pray for favor from God and man as Jesus found favor with both so can we find favor with both (Luke 2:52; Exodus 12:36). You can give others hope and build them up in their most holy faith by agreeing with them and prophesying over them, exhorting them to believe in the destiny and plan God has for their lives and thereby supporting them in their vision.

THE ESSENCE OF HOPE

You find hope in God and hope in God's Word. God places hope in your heart before you even really know him. Hope is that *energizing force* that keeps you moving ever forward and closer to God, the source of all hope. God gives hope in his Word. You can bring hope into actual substance by speaking God's Word in all circumstances. You choose to speak God's Word rather than your words of defeat thereby choosing life. Though speech, you subject your most unruly member (your tongue) into agreement with Creator God and gain control over the physical realm. As you persist in this action the physical circumstances around you have to conform to God's Word. Literally you are changing the physical world into the Kingdom through the words of your mouth. Praising in all circumstances is another powerful means to take physical ground (Romans 8:28).

CHAPTER FIVE OVERVIEW: LIFE OR DEATH

God's Kingdom is a Kingdom where you have choices: Love is a choice, faith is a choice, and hope is a choice. You choose and follow forward with persistence until you find how God would use those choices. In choosing to love you have discovered the heartbeat of the Kingdom. In choosing faith you make the substance, calling into being those things that were not. In choosing hope you plug into the energizing force of the Kingdom. God did not make these principles to make your life difficult. Rather, God knows that as you put into practice these principles you will truly realize freedom - a freedom and a joy you never even knew existed.

God's Kingdom is not a Kingdom built on natural law neither is it earned by natural law. (Important: Read Galatians chapter three.) His is a spiritual Kingdom built on spiritual principles. You make Kingdom choices in the supernatural and then what you have acquired in the supernatural becomes substance in the natural. It becomes substance for you and for your family. You participate in the Kingdom as you exercise your freewill and call forth the Kingdom, and continue to call forth the Kingdom.

In not making any choices, or knowing about the choices but not really seizing them for yourself, you stay under the sentence of death and the curse. Why would you want to stay there when faith sets you free? Therefore, with the choice of your lips choose this day, life or death, blessing or cursing. It is entirely your choice. Beginning this very day, let it be said of you, you have chosen wisely.

Throughout Chapter Five, choices, principles and actions are placed before you to reveal the Kingdom. Know that the examples given are not the only ways the Spirit works. As you apply these teachings, they will open your eyes to the freedom of God's Kingdom living and the Spirit will open your eyes to any additional principles he wants you to learn. It is your faith journey.

CHAPTER 6   KINGDOM HEALTH PLAN
INTRODUCTION   HEALING FOR THE BODY AND SOUL

HEALING FOR BODY AND SOUL

Man is a triune creature: body, soul and spirit. The body is the physical, outward appearance; the soul includes the mind, will and emotions; and the spirit is where the Spirit of God resides. The Kingdom Health Plan addresses each area.

Spiritual healing has been addressed in this text through breaking generational curses, cutting soul ties, and forgiveness. This kind of healing is also addressed further in deliverance in the Kingdom text, Christian Primary III, The Power. The following sections address physical healing and inner healing.

PART 1   JOY AND WISDOM AS A MEDICINE

Proverbs 17:22 states, *A cheerful heart is good medicine, but a crushed spirit dries up the bones*. God has prescribed a large dose of his medicine for his children, and that medicine is to be cheerful. Those who enter into that cheer, even if they are not quite sure how this medicine works will receive the benefits - because the Word of God is true.

Joy is medicine for the body, just as laughter and songs of joy are part of deliverance (Psalm 126:1-6). God uses laughter as he routs the enemy (Psalm 2:4). Joy is an anointing (Psalm 45:7). We are filled with joy at the presence of God (Psalm 16:11). The presence of the Lord is the greatest blessing and the well-spring of all other blessings. If we are dwelling in the presence of the Lord we dwell in joy (Psalm 21:6).

Trust in the Lord with all your heart, lean not unto your own understanding. In all your ways acknowledge him, and he will make your paths straight.

Do not be wise in your own eyes; Fear the Lord and shun evil. This will bring health to your body and nourishment to your bones (Proverbs 3:5-8).

PART 2   HEALING FOR THE PHYSICAL BODY

All disease originates with sin. In the garden with Adam and Eve, there was no disease, no deadly virus, no bacteria, no illness, no infections, no bugs, no germs. Through the disobedience of the first man, Adam, a door was flung open and in marched disease and death. The killer is not cancer, hepatitis, aides, heart attacks; the killer is sin.

The second Adam, Jesus, came to restore what the first Adam lost. Through an act of obedience, Jesus laid down his life as a blood sacrifice to pay for the restoration of the Kingdom. He paid for sin and now death and disease have their marching orders. Sin is the disease, the curse. In the Kingdom you can exchange the curse for the blessing of life.

When Jesus Christ is your Lord and Savior, you enter into eternal life. When you accept him as Healer you enter into health. Jesus has come and healing is his song. You obtain this song by learning to be a singer yourself. Persist until you become one with the song and one with the singer. The song of the Kingdom is healing, the song is one of the greatest gifts of love for it is a song of his love - God loving us while we are yet sinners. As you receive healing, apply a generous amount of wisdom. If you are taking a prescription or are under a Doctors care, return to the Doctor and have him confirm your healing.

Know it is the will of the King for those in his Kingdom to be in good health.

THE KINGDOM HEALTH PLAN: GOD HEALS* TO DISPLAY HIS GLORY JOHN 9:3

♦ God heals through Love (Love is the heart and heartbeat of the Kingdom). God so loved the world he gave his only Son that you might receive and practice forgiveness: forgive others, yourself, confess sin and receive forgiveness. He gave us anointing with oil for forgiveness of sins (James 5:14-16) He heals our mind, our will and our emotions. You receive healing because Jesus took upon himself your infirmities, and by his stripes you are healed (Isaiah 53:4-5, Matthew 8:17).

◆ God heals through Faith, making substance of the Kingdom in your life. You take things in the spiritual realm and pull them into the realm of the natural. Faith in action is seizing the Covenants and walking in Covenant promises, thereby loosing healing and binding up disease. You practice faith in inner healing and deliverance and through the gifts of the Spirit (deliverance and gifts are covered in Christian Primary III, The Power).

◆ God heals through Hope, the energizing force of the Kingdom, intercession, signs and wonders, and words of prophecy. Using *positive Kingdom speak* (praise, God' Words, positive attitude) to take the Kingdom, speaking the Word of God in all circumstances (prophesying to yourself), thereby taking control of and in the physical realm. Controlling the mouth and the tongue thereby controlling the whole body. God provides miraculous healing through natural remedies (2 Kings 20:7) wisdom, laughter and joy.

PART 3 INNER HEALING

Inner healing can also be called emotional healing or healing for the soul. It is a process whereby difficult memories are brought to the conscious level. There, Jesus heals the memory. The memory then can be recalled, but it is no longer accompanied by pain, but accompanied by the signs and wonders.

The most powerful healing happens as you place yourself in the hands of Jesus and ask him to reveal areas of your soul needing healing. Find a quiet place and a time and just ask and wait and watch. As a memory is recalled, ask Jesus and the Holy Spirit to walk with you through your memory, healing you where you need healing. Invite Jesus to hold your hand as you review the hurt and the pain. Watch, wait, and listen to Jesus and the Holy Spirit as they speak to your heart and reveal pictures of healing in your mind.

Not all inner healing needs to happen this way, however, this is one very powerful approach to open yourself to inner healing. God knows you, including your deepest needs. He formed you in the womb and called you by name: he has carved you on the palms of his hands

(Jeremiah 1:5). God has chosen you, you did not choose him. He is interested in healing you and restoring your soul! *

The following pages suggest areas in which people may need inner healing for their inner being. Basic information is included to help direct your prayers. Read Ephesians 3:14-19. Notice how God wishes to strengthen you in your inner man.

*If healing and change do not occur another direction to explore is deliverance. A through study of deliverance can be found in, Christian Primary III, The Power.

THE HEART

The heart is deceitful, often hiding its true nature and feelings. Ask the Holy Spirit to reveal what is hidden in your heart so you can pray, confess your sin and receive healing. Ask God to give you a new heart. (Ezekiel 36:24-26). Write the teachings of the Lord on the tablet of your heart (Proverbs 7:1-3).

ABANDONMENT

When a child is abandoned, he or she will suffer a spiritual hole in their heart - an area that becomes open for deception. It is like a howling emptiness, as torment has been allowed access to the heart. Pray for the abandoned heart to be restored and healed. Because this person can consistently make poor choices in relationships, pray that discernment will be restored to the heart and that it will be protected. Pray forgiveness. Face the torment and in the name of Jesus command it to leave. Psalm 147:3 teaches, God heals the broken-hearted and will bind up their wounds.

THE BROKEN HEART

A heart that has been hurt repeatedly will find it difficult to feel and accept love no matter how much love is given. A person in this situation needs to have prayer for their heart to be healed so they may receive love.

God is close to those with a broken heart and will heal them (Psalm 34:18, 147:3).

WALLS

Because of hurt, you can begin to build interior walls of safety for protection from further hurt. You can reach out and love, but you are prevented from really believing you are loved. These inside protective barriers prevent love from entering. These walls prevent you from growing up. Emotional development stops at the point where walls were established. Your emotions are trapped behind those walls. The real you is trapped behind those walls. On the outside where everyone can view you, you present a mask to hide your hurt. Inside you are trapped in a dark cave.

This *hiding place* was a place of safety as you lived through hurt - a way of coping with difficult circumstances and emotions when you knew of no other. But now you need to be set free. What can you do? First, pray for freedom by: recognizing and/or admitting the walls, forgive those who contributed to the building of your walls, and ask for healing. Visualize Jesus coming to help you remove your walls. See Jesus take your hand and lead you out of the dark place into his light. You will sense that person you really wanted to be (who was trapped inside) free to be completely expressed. You are emotionally, free!

Your emotions can be pretty unpredictable once freed. It will be a bit intimidating to allow your trapped emotions free. You will have to learn anew how to manage them.

You will also become vulnerable to people and hurt. If you choose not to be vulnerable you will not experience those deep emotions of being loved. *You will be hurt again and again,* but now you can deal with that hurt. It's a choice to come out from behind these walls. Once you know this process you may see yourself building back those walls. Freedom is on the outside and it is safe there with Jesus. Ask Jesus to reveal you walls and then actively participate in keeping your walls down.

REJECTION FROM BIRTH

When a mother does not want her child and/or considers having an abortion, the child experiences that rejection (Psalm 27:10). This root of rejection and bitterness forms in the heart of the child. There can even be a sense of death or wanting to die. That spirit of rejection (visible in anger and bitterness) needs prayer and the command to depart. The root of bitterness needs to be confessed and then commanded to loose its grip and leave. Pray against a spirit of murder if abortion was considered. Truth needs to be placed into the spirit of the child so they know they are wanted and have been called forth from the womb by God. God chooses them and they are to choose life (1 Peter 2:9-11).

BITTERNESS/BITTER ROOTS

Bitterness takes root when a person is hurt by broken promises or broken relationships. Pray, commanding any roots of bitterness to shrivel up and die (Ephesians 4:31). Choose to be rooted and established in love (Ephesians 3:17). When you receive this kind of prayer, you may experience a spitting up or bitter taste in your mouth.

A BROKEN SPIRIT

Divorce in a family can produce a broken spirit in a child. Their emotional growth stops. Recognize the broken area, stand and forgive, and pray for the broken spirit to be healed. Know that it can be difficult to be faithful in their marriage, as divorce is always that *easy option*.

Divorce robs the child and they are thrown into a barren place where there are constant tormenting spirits. This barrenness is not easily recognized because it becomes so familiar. In this place a tormenting spirit constantly drives them. And in this barren land lives the Dragon (Spirit of Jealously). It is he who constantly tears up their lives and destroys all the good they would plant. This is an area for deliverance as well as inner healing. See *Christian Primary III, The Power*, under, *The Spirit of Jealously*, to break this hold. Recommended reading is *The Rumors of Nard*.

This does not mean a parent should stay in a relationship where there is physical or sexual abuse just to avoid divorce. God can restore and give a new beginning for he is the God of New Beginnings. He is also the God of all knowledge, so ask him for wisdom in how to proceed and he will be faithful to guide and direct you.

SHAME

The soul experiences shame for various reasons, most especially because of sexual abuse. It can also be for loss of job, position, others sinning in your family, or personal sin. In these situations, pray for the soul to be healed, forgiveness, the removal of anger, the healing of pain, and the shame to be removed from you and your family. (Romans 9:33).

In Isaiah 61:7 there is found a precious promise for those who have experienced shame. They receive the double portion: *Instead of their shame my people will receive a double portion, instead of disgrace they will rejoice in their inheritance and so they will inherit a double portion in their land and everlasting joy will be theirs.*

THE BREACH

The seeds of disrespect can be sown into family members. Seeds of distrust may be planted into children because a wife disrespects her husband. As a result, the children do not honor their parents and lack respect for them. This breakdown of respect can follow generational lines, preventing the children from having a healthy, intimate relationship with their parents.

This sin of disrespect and dishonor needs to be repented of and replaced with respect. Pray over the seeds of disrespect so they will no longer produce a negative harvest. Scripture teaches that whatever is sown will be reaped.

GUILT

Guilt can be heavy emotional baggage, resulting from sin, inappropriate feelings of responsibility for a wrong (such as a divorce, a teenager's rebellion, loss of a job), or because others perceive us as guilty. For actual wrongs committed, sincerely ask for (and receive) God's forgiveness. Receiving God's forgiveness allows us to stop judging ourselves and let go of the guilt (1 John 1:7-9).

If others perceive you as guilty and you are not, treat it as a judgment and command their judgment of you to be broken.

THE SLUMBERING SPIRIT

At times a person can know God and have received salvation but perhaps due to devastation, rebellion, loss of vision and dreams, drugs, hanging out with the wrong crowd, their spirit (where the Spirit of the Lord helps them discern) goes to asleep. They do not respond to the Gospel or have dreams or visions. They do not look around and perceive that they are lost and asleep. They need God's forgiveness (Romans 10:14).

Pray that the slumbering spirit awake. Command it to awake. Command the plugs out of the ears. Command the blinders off of the eyes. Command the soul (intellect, will and emotions) to respond to the Spirit of God (Ephesians 5:13-15).

DEATH

If people have not moved though a normal grieving process, cried, sensed the loss, experienced the anger, accepted and received the healing and assurance of God in death or loss, they can take on a great heaviness in their heart.

As a young child, I was unaware of the grieving process. Not knowing what my future held, I could not let down my defenses and grieve for the death of my mother and the break-up of my parents' marriage. In my subconscious I held on the that moment and never grew emotionally beyond it. As I grew older I developed violent allergies.

One day, after many unsuccessful Doctor treatments, I was driving down the road and the Lord spoke to me. He revealed I had suppressed my grief and heaviness and was holding on to my mother and that was the weight and also why I was experiencing the allergy attacks. I immediately confessed and asked forgiveness and prayed that I would be released from my mother. A huge weight rolled off my chest.

On rare occasion I still have problems with allergies but they are more head symptoms and never serious enough to need Doctor treatment.

I have prayed for another where, in the spirit, I viewed a large black cloud of depression over them. I prayed to set them from grief and depression. Literally they saw light fill the room as everything got brighter and their heart felt full of light.

LIVE THE KINGDOM

For the moment our journey together into knowing God's Kingdom ends. However, your journey to truly know God and his Kingdom is only beginning. Let not your journey be one of just faithful obedience but also a true journey of the heart and relationship. Live with great expectation, spontaneity and joy. Lend your ear to the Holy Spirit to be your daily guide and you will always find the pathway true and full of adventure. God bless you as you continually make the Kingdom choice and set your feet and your mind and your heart upon his path. God truly rewards those who love him with an outrageous love and who diligently seek after him.

For the Kingdom,

Ginny

Order these Great Books from the Kingdom Series

The Kingdom - CHRISTIAN PRIMARY I

God has a Kingdom. His desire is that his Kingdom be established on earth as it is in heaven. This text gives a comprehensive overview of God's Kingdom and offers practical suggestions on how to enter into Kingdom living. It includes: basic Kingdom structure, practical applications of faith, love and hope, and concludes with a study on physical and inner healing. ISBN 0-9718325-0-1 $13.00

The Glory - CHRISTIAN PRIMARY II

Jesus is the Glory! He is the light of the world. Light contains all color. Here in this Kingdom coloring book, *The Glory,* explore colors, numbers and spiritual gifts using color as a visual aide. Man was created to walk in the light of the glory of God. Available Fall, 2003. ISBN 0-9718325-1-X $13.00

The Power - CHRISTIAN PRIMARY III

The Holy Spirit is the Power - the gift from God the Father - the teacher and guide to all truth! This text offers a practical study of how to enter into a relationship with the Holy Spirit and how to practice deliverance. Negative color charts reveal how evil spirits operate. Available Fall, 2003. ISBN 0-9718325-2-8 $13.00

The Kingdom - TEACHER'S MANUAL

A teacher's manual to teach the Bible Study, *The Kingdom.* Developed by a veteran teacher, this easy to use teacher's guide, offers 15 pages of chapter-by-chapter study guides, 15 pages of ready to use hands-on activities, and the compete text of *The Kingdom.* It includes a treasure map and art front plates of the four Gospels. Available spring of 2004. ISBN 0-9718325-3-6 $26.00

Order on-line at Amazon.com, or for orders of 50 or more contact
EvenSong Publishing for discounts. **Phone (503) 325-4621**
EvenSong Publishing, 1438 Jerome Ave., Astoria, Oregon 97103

EvenSong Publishing, 1438 Jerome Ave., Astoria, Oregon 97103
"Publishing the good news for the New Millennium"